Gardens *of the* Roman World

Gardens *of the* Roman World

PATRICK BOWE

THE J. PAUL GETTY MUSEUM, LOS ANGELES

CONTENTS

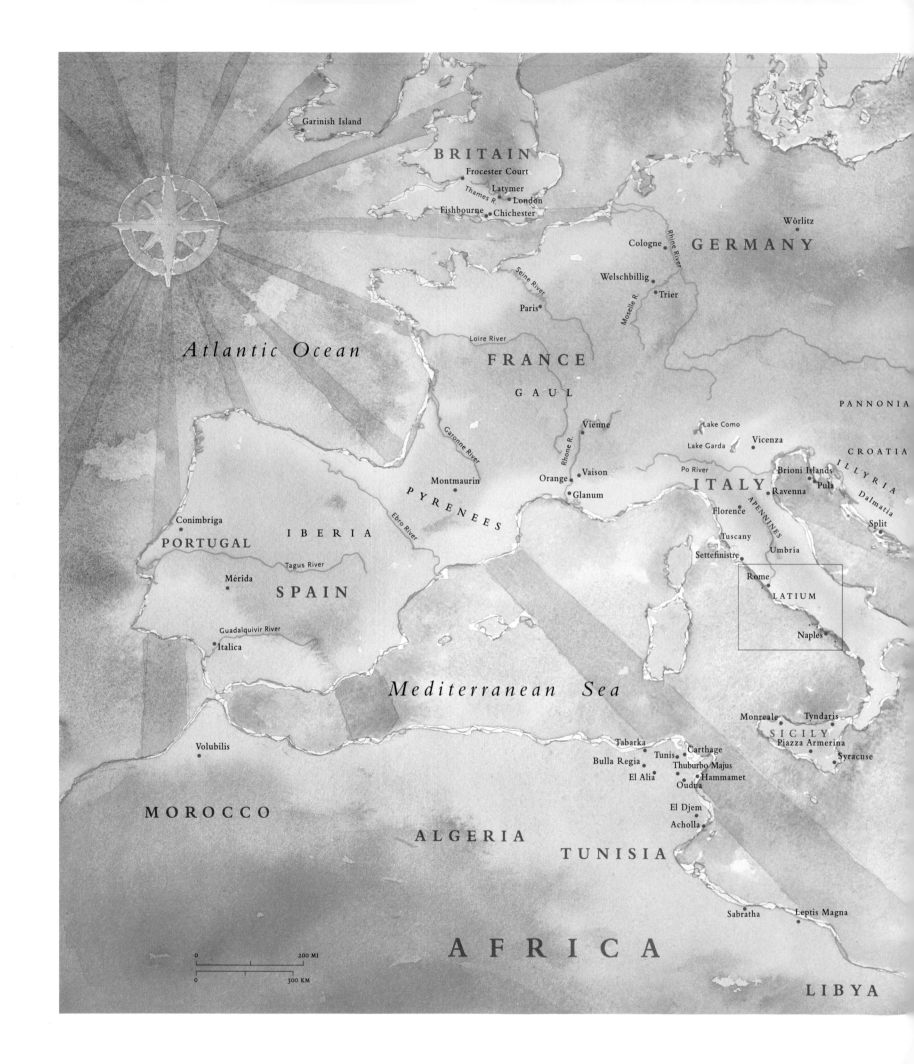

BRITAIN

Garinish Island

Frocester Court

Latymer

Thames R.

London

Fishbourne

Chichester

GERMANY

Wörlitz

Cologne

Rhine River

Welschbillig

Moselle R.

Trier

Seine River

Paris

Loire River

FRANCE

GAUL

Atlantic Ocean

PANNONIA

Vienne

Lake Como

Vicenza

Lake Garda

CROATIA

ILLYRIA

Rhone R.

Caronne River

Po River

Orange

Vaison

ITALY

Brioni Islands

Pula

Dalmatia

Montmaurin

PYRENEES

Glanum

Ravenna

Split

Conimbriga

Ebro River

Florence

APENNINES

PORTUGAL

IBERIA

Tuscany

Umbria

Tagus River

Settefinistre

Mérida

Rome

Italica

SPAIN

LATIUM

Guadalquivir River

Naples

Mediterranean Sea

Volubilis

Monreale

Tyndaris

SICILY

Piazza Armerina

Syracuse

Tabarka

Carthage

Tunis

Bulla Regia

Thuburbo Majus

El Alia

Hammamet

Oudna

MOROCCO

El Djem

Acholla

ALGERIA

TUNISIA

AFRICA

Sabratha

Leptis Magna

0   200 MI

0   300 KM

LIBYA

SABINE HILLS

Licenza

Tivoli

Tiber River

Rome

Praeneste

Frascati

Ostia

Castel

ALBAN HILLS

Gandolfo

Lake Nemi

Arpinum

Laurentum

LATIUM

CAMPAGNA

Sperlonga

Gaeta

Herculaneum

MOUNT VESUVIUS

Cumae

Naples

Boscoreale

Murecine

Boscotrecase

Oplontis

Pompeii

Stabiae

Bay of Naples

Sorrento

Capri

Paestum

Aquincum

Budapest

HUNGARY

Black Sea

Danube River

Constantinople

MOUNT OLYMPUS

MOUNT IDA

TURKEY

Aegean Sea

THESSALY

Corfu

GREECE

Athens

Aphrodisias

Euphrates River

Tigris River

Delos

Cyclades

Kameiros

Rhodes

Dura-Europos

Rhodes

SYRIA

Damascus

Mediterranean Sea

Jericho

Dead Sea

Cyrene

Masada

JORDAN

Alexandria

EGYPT

Nile R.

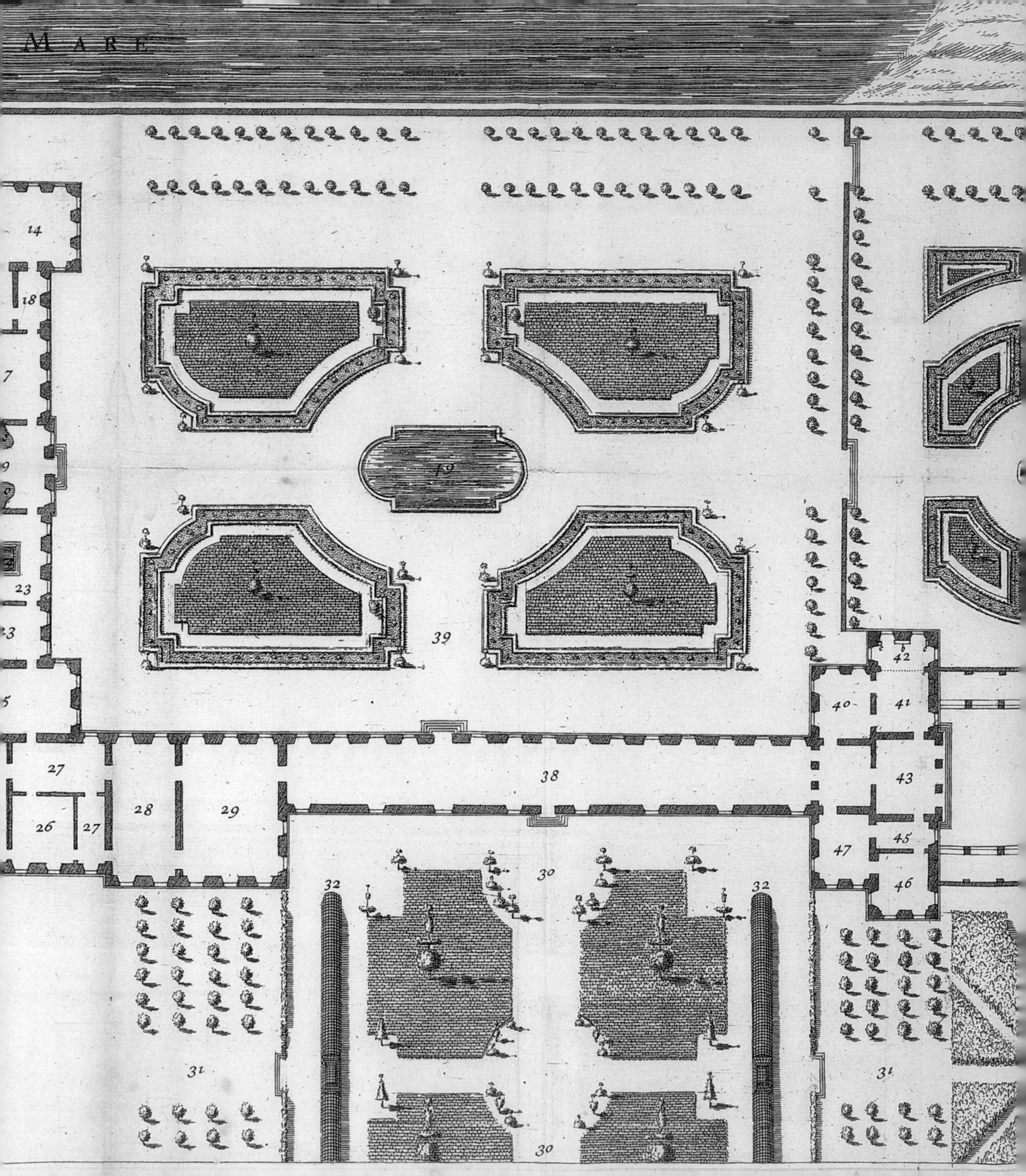
MARE
14
18
7
9
23
3
5
27
26
27
28
29
38
39
49
40
41
42
43
45
46
47
30
32
32
31
31
30

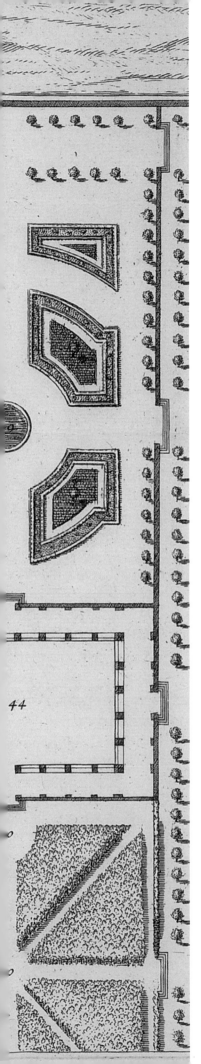

I

THE ROMAN GARDEN: AN INTRODUCTION

ROMAN GARDENS, in their conception, style, and planting, were inspired by the earlier gardens of the Near East, Egypt, and Greece. In their turn, Roman gardens influenced the great Italian gardens of the Renaissance, the early nineteenth-century Neoclassical gardens of the Western world, as well as twentieth-century gardens in England, France, and the United States, most notably the garden at the J. Paul Getty Museum in Malibu, California. Roman gardens are an essential part of the continuum that is the garden history of the Western world.

Plan of the garden of Pliny's seaside Laurentine villa. Many visualizations of Pliny's gardens have been made over the years based on the descriptions in his *Letters*. Some reflect more the garden style of the period when the visualization was made than that of the true garden style of ancient Rome. For example, this drawing appears to be a plan of a typical seventeenth-century French Baroque garden. From Jean-François Félibien des Avaux, *Les plans et les descriptions de deux des plus belles maisons de campagne de Pliné le consul* (Paris, 1699), p. 9. 14, mid-sized dining room; 30, gardens; 31, grand tree-lined road; 32, trellis; 38, closed gallery; 39, exercise area; 40, solarium; 44, courtyard for men; 49, wellhead or fountain. At the top of the plan is the sea (*mare*).

We know that many of the elements characteristic of ancient Roman gardens had been featured in Mesopotamian gardens from the fifteenth century B.C. Tree-planted courtyards with stone-edged pools and pavilions set among flower and vegetable beds were already present along the banks of the Euphrates River at this early date. However, the influence of Mesopotamian gardens was indirect, filtered through the later gardening traditions of Persia, Greece, and Egypt.

HISTORICAL BACKGROUND

The Persian Influence • Narrow water canals or rills graced many gardens in ancient Rome. The best-known example is in the garden of Loreius Tiburtinus in Pompeii (fig. 1; see also figs. 95–96). Many centuries earlier, such rills had been the organizing feature of Persian gardens. Their abundance in the gardens of the Persian royal palace complex at Pasar-gadae and at other sites must have struck the soldiers of Alexander the Great's army when they swept through Persia in 330 B.C. Although no rills have been excavated in the gardens of Classical Greece, knowledge of them was surely transmitted to Rome through the Greeks. The narrow canals featured in Roman gardens were sometimes called *euripes* after the Euripus, the narrow channel between the island of Euboea and mainland Greece.

The Egyptian Influence • The Romans also knew and admired the ancient gardening traditions of Egypt. The Egyptians had irrigated their gardens for centuries by means of specially constructed water channels. Their knowledge of hydraulics was advanced, and they had constructed extensive terraces long before the Assyrian people startled the world with their terraced Hanging Gardens of Babylon. In fact, Egyptian garden designers anticipated many of the features traditionally associated with the Roman garden—a symmetrical layout with water features, brightly painted pavilions, terraces, and avenues of trees. Atrium gardens, or gardens in internal courtyards, which we have long associated with the city of Pompeii, had been laid out in Egypt many centuries before.

Egyptian influence on Rome could also be seen in great Roman gardens with areas designed expressly to recall some of Egypt's legendary places. Cicero mocked the pretensions of those Romans who created extensive garden water features in deliberate mimicry of the river Nile. At his villa at Tivoli, near Rome, the emperor Hadrian (r. A.D. 117–138) created a canal in imitation of the well-known canalized branch of the Nile at the Egyptian pleasure resort of Canopus (fig. 2; see also fig. 64). Furthermore, he had pastiche Egyptian and Greek statuary erected along the edge of his "Canopus." The Romans had imported much antique Egyptian statuary after Egypt became a province of Rome in 30 B.C.

The Greek Influence • The principal Greek influence on the Roman garden was on its architecture. The Greeks began using the portico, or colonnade, as an intermediary space between house and garden in the fourth century B.C., and this technique was later adapted by the Romans. The earliest use of such colonnades at Pompeii, for example, dates to the second century B.C. After this date the gardens of Roman town houses were often surrounded by covered colonnades known as "peristyles," and the gardens of Roman country villas boasted porticoes that were open to the surrounding view. As Romans looked to Greece for their artistic inspiration, they often decorated their gardens with Greek or Greek-inspired sculptures. This was particularly so after the Romans conquered Greece in 146 B.C., when Greek sculptures and other works of art flooded into Rome along with Greek sculptors seeking commissions.

The art of the ornamental garden was also imported from Greece, the earliest known pleasure gardens in Rome being those of military commanders such as Licinius Lucullus (d. 57/56 B.C.), who had fought in and experienced the Greek world. It is significant that the famous Roman writer Cicero (106–43 B.C.) used words of Greek derivation, such as *topiarius* and *ars topiaria* for "gardener" and "gardening." Greek gardeners emigrated to Rome to find new patrons after the Roman conquest of Greece. They brought with them their gardening art as well as their practical horticultural techniques, which were then developed over time. Subsequently, gardening played a much bigger part in Roman life than it ever had in Greece due to the strong agrarian roots of the citizens of Rome.

Fig. 1.
The House of Loreius Tiburtinus, Pompeii. This house's garden featured an extensive canal. This view looks from the upper arm of the canal to the lower through the architectural superstructure of the fountain, which marks the junction of the canal's two arms. Rows of postholes on either side of the lower canal arm were found to have the cavities of vine roots nearby, a discovery that led to the conjectural reconstruction of the vine pergolas seen in the garden today. (See also fig. 95.)

Fig. 2.
Hadrian's Villa, Tivoli. The emperor Hadrian spent much time traveling and was heavily influenced by the eastern part of his empire. When he began to design his country villa near Tivoli, he included a water feature called the Canopus after the canalized river of that name in Egypt.

THE DEVELOPMENT OF THE ROMAN GARDEN

The Roman garden synthesized elements from the above traditions, crystallizing them into a view of the garden as an art form that was to become a hallmark of Western culture.

The earliest records of the ornamental garden on Italian soil date from the third century B.C. At that time, the Greek rulers of Syracuse, on the island of Sicily, had hunting parks. One such park contained an Amaltheion, a sanctuary dedicated to the nymph Amalthea (see "Grottoes and Nymphaea," pp. 24–25). It was ornamented by a grove of trees, some pools of water, and a grotto. Hieron II, a ruler of Syracuse, is known to have had a garden laid out on his boat so that he could enjoy the pleasures of a garden at sea. Among the earliest recorded Roman colonnaded, or peristyle, gardens are those at Pompeii, dating from the second century B.C. However, the peak period of classical gardening in Italy was later, stretching approximately from 150 B.C. to A.D. 350.

Gardens of the Roman Republic (ca. 150 – 27 B.C.) •
At the end of the second century B.C., most
Roman gardens were still kitchen gardens.
However, by the next century, a few ornamental
villa gardens were being established on the hills
around the city of Rome. On the Pincian Hill
in Rome, the great military commander Licinius
Lucullus had a garden designed to provide a
splendid setting for his famous feasts. The garden
overlooked the green spaces of the public park
known as the Campus Martius, the Field of Mars.
The top terrace of Lucullus's garden was in the
form of a walled semicircle studded with statuary
niches, from which monumental flights of steps
descended through a series of terraces to an
artificial lake below. On the lake, Lucullus sometimes arranged mock naval battles for the entertainment of his guests. Also established at this
time was the luxurious garden of the navy commander and writer Sallust (86–35 B.C.), which
was located in a valley between the Pincian and
Quirinal Hills. It too consisted of architecturally
planned terraces. These were laid out around a
domed pavilion that Sallust had erected above
a natural spring.

No direct evidence survives of the planting
of these luxurious gardens. However, it is known
that during Lucullus's military campaigns in the
east, he introduced the edible cherry (*Prunus cerasus*) from the Kingdom of Pontus (a region located in present-day Turkey) to Rome. It is probable
that other exotic plants from the east were beginning to appear in Roman gardens alongside
native species.

Little remains of these late republican
gardens—we know about them only from texts
and inscriptions. During the imperial period,
these gardens were annexed by the emperors for
their own use, and some were later willed for
public use, as was Caesar's garden located west

of the Tiber River in Rome near the area known
today as Trastevere. This was the garden in which
he is said to have received Cleopatra shortly
before his death, in 44 B.C.

Gardens of the Roman Empire (27 B.C.– ca. A.D. 350) •
With the collapse of the Roman Republic and
the advent of the Roman Empire in 27 B.C., luxurious gardens became more widespread, every
imperial and aristocratic family having one. The
grandest gardens, as one might expect, were those
of the emperors. Among the best-known imperial
gardens were those of the official palaces on one
of Rome's hills, the Palatine Hill (from which the
word "palace" derives). They were most remarkable under the emperor Domitian (r. A.D. 81–96)
during the first century A.D. Also famous was the
short-lived garden and park of the emperor
Nero's Golden House, which was constructed
about A.D. 64. Among imperial country gardens,
Domitian's at Castel Gandolfo, near Rome, and
those of the emperor Hadrian at Tivoli in the
second century A.D. were the most noteworthy.
Not so much gardens as huge complexes of gardens, their spaces interlocked with the villas'
buildings in an integral way.

Many imperial and aristocratic families had
more than one villa and garden. They moved
from one to another according to the seasons of
the year. They might have had a city garden in
Rome, a villa garden in the nearby Alban Hills, a
seaside villa garden on the coast between Rome
and Naples, a garden on the family's agricultural
estate in the fertile Campagna (rural plain region)
south of Rome, and a garden in yet another part
of Italy, such as Tuscany.

Gradually, the Roman garden style was disseminated throughout the empire, from Portugal
in the west (fig. 3) to Syria in the east, from
Britain and Germany in the north to Egypt in
the south. The style's influence reached beyond
the empire in the east, eventually being seminal
in the development of the Islamic garden style.
Even after the transfer of the empire's capital from
Rome to Constantinople after A.D. 324, Roman
aristocrats continued to make gardens in the west,
the tradition ending only with the collapse of the
Western Empire in the late fifth century.

Fig. 3.
The House of the Swastikas, Conimbriga, Portugal. This
courtyard garden with its pool and formal island beds is
surrounded by a colonnade and by rooms renowned for
their complex geometric mosaics. (See also figs. 158 – 59.)

SOURCES

Our knowledge of Roman gardens is based on four sources: literary testimony, archaeological evidence, pictorial records, and horticultural traditions.

Literary Testimony • Four great agricultural treatises were compiled in ancient Rome. Although these works are mainly about farming, they also contain a wealth of information about the practice of gardening. The first, authored by Cato the Censor (234–149 B.C.), was entitled *De agricultura* (On agriculture), although a later translation used the title *De re rustica* (On rural affairs). *De re rustica* was the title used for the other three treatises, authored by Varro (116–27 B.C.), Columella (mid-first century A.D.), and Palladius (fourth century A.D.). Palladius's book enjoyed popularity for centuries due to his arrangement of gardening advice according to the months of the year, in what is known as "gardener's calendar" form. In addition to these four treatises, *Historia naturalis* (Natural history), the encyclopedia of Pliny the Elder (A.D. ca. 23–79), has always been a primary source of information on Roman gardens. It includes sections on botany as well as agriculture, horticulture, and medical matters.

However, these works give little information about Roman garden design or ornamentation. Our knowledge of these aspects of gardening comes only from other, scattered literary sources. Foremost among them are the *Letters* of Pliny the Younger (A.D. ca. 61–ca. 113), in which he described in some detail the design and ornamental planting of two of his villas. One was his villa on the coast near Ostia, southwest of Rome (see p. 2); it was located at Vicus Augustanus Laurentium, usually referred to by the shorter name of Laurentum. The other villa was in Tuscany, in a place then known as Tifernum Tiberinum. (The site is now occupied by the town of Città di Castello, which, due to regional boundary changes, is now located in Umbria. For uniformity, it will continue to be referred to as Tuscan in this book.)

Archaeological Evidence • Archaeological research has provided much detailed information about Roman garden design and planting. Research into ancient Rome and its buildings was begun in the fifteenth century, during the Renaissance. Although only fragments of ancient gardens then remained, those of Domitian's palace on the Palatine Hill and of Hadrian's Villa at Tivoli were a fruitful source of ideas for Renaissance garden designers.

With the discovery and excavation in the eighteenth century of the ancient cities of Herculaneum and Pompeii, more extensive knowledge of ancient Roman gardens became available. Vesuvius's eruption in A.D. 79 engulfed Pompeii in a layer of ash and lapilli, under which the traces of hundreds of gardens were protected—an unparalleled resource for the study of garden history. Only at Pompeii can garden development be traced over a continuous period of almost four hundred years, from the end of the fourth century B.C. to A.D. 79. To this day, excavations continue to reveal exciting finds.

Our knowledge has also been increased by excavations of archaeological sites in outlying or provincial parts of the ancient Roman world. Within western Europe, excavations in Britain, France, Portugal, and Spain have uncovered the remains of many Roman villas and their gardens. Similarly fruitful excavations have taken place in North Africa, particularly in Morocco, Libya, and Tunisia. In the Near East, notably in Syria, much information about gardens has been uncovered, and in central European countries such as Hungary and Croatia, the remains of large-scale Roman villas have been investigated and the details of their gardens revealed.

Until a century ago, archaeologists paid more attention to ancient buildings than to the gardens that surrounded them. In the process, many garden sites and their remains have been damaged. At first, modern garden excavations tended to focus on a garden's structure or hard landscaping, such as its pools, paths, and other elements of architecture, neglecting the plantings. However, contemporary analyses are focusing for the first time on garden soils, which contain seed and root remains that provide extensive information on plants and planting.

Pictorial Records • Much useful information about Roman gardens can be derived from pictorial representations that have survived on the walls and floors of excavated Roman buildings. However, caution may be needed when scanning them for detail because the information may not be fully accurate. The artist may have taken artistic license in the interpretation of the subject. Pictorial records of Roman gardens survive in two different artistic media: frescoes, which are paintings mainly located on wall surfaces (fig. 4), and mosaics, which are pictures composed of small pieces of stone and which are mainly seen on floor surfaces.

The frescoes that are of interest from a garden point of view are usually in one of two categories: (A) those with a garden theme and (B) those with a broader rural landscape theme:
A.   Garden theme frescoes (figs. 5–7). In ancient Rome, the walls of houses, both inside and out, and the walls of gardens were often decorated with mural paintings depicting gardens. Interior mural paintings were conceived as a way of giving a room an outdoor, or "garden," atmosphere. Wall-paintings of this type were typical of the houses in Pompeii but could also be enjoyed in the grand imperial villas of Rome, such as the House of Livia, wife of the first emperor, Augustus, which was located just outside Rome. Exterior wall-paintings, on the other hand, were contrived to make a small garden appear larger than it was. In both cases, the aim was achieved with the use of a painting technique now known as "trompe l'oeil." Used since ancient Egyptian times, this form of painting produces an illusion of reality so as "to deceive the eye" (see fig. 25). Equally informative are small decorative paintings that make up continuous friezes around the walls of a room above the main mural paintings. These often show, in miniaturized form, details of garden structures such as pergolas, arbors, fences, seats, and vases arranged in formal designs.

Fig. 4.

Fresco from the House of the Golden Bracelet, Pompeii (also known as the House of Alexander's Wedding). This wall fresco, one of the most refined of all Pompeian frescoes, was discovered in 1979. It leaves the spectator with the impression of standing on the edge of a garden. It depicts that combination of art and nature typical of the best Roman gardens, in which sculptural pieces are integrally associated with the garden's plants. Here, gilded busts on pedestals support low-relief panels of reclining figures, and a delicately carved, fluted basin contains a burbling fountain. Also depicted in the fresco is a pair of theatrical masks suspended from the crossbar of a pergola. Such masks were known as *oscilli* because their suspension on chains allowed them to swing back and forth, or oscillate. The vegetation is painted with accuracy and gives us a comprehensive picture of a typical Pompeian garden planting. Trees and shrubs such as oriental plane (*Platanus orientalis*), arbutus (*Arbutus unedo*), bay laurel (*Laurus nobilis*), and laurustinus (*Viburnum tinus*) are depicted with date palms (*Phoenix dactylifera*), oleander (*Nerium oleander*), and roses (*Rosa* sp.). Smaller flowering plants like chamomile (*Chamaemelum nobile*), marigold (*Calendula officinalis*), opium poppy (*Papaver somniferum*), iris (*Iris* sp.), hart's-tongue fern (*Phyllitis scolopendrium*), and ivy, both plain and variegated (*Hedera* sp.), are also shown.

Fig. 5. ◁
Fresco detail from the House of the
Golden Bracelet, Pompeii. A magpie
perches on a bay laurel, and a white
fan-tailed pigeon is about to alight
on a laurustinus, a shrub with close,
flat clusters of white flowers. A
panel known as a *pinax* depicts
a reclining goddess painted in realistic colors.

Fig. 6. ▷
Fresco detail from the House of
the Golden Bracelet, Pompeii. A
decorative stone shaft is topped
with a gilded mask representing
Pan, who was a god of the countryside and thus appropriate for representation in a garden. The tree
with fruit is the strawberry tree, the
native *Arbutus unedo*. The flowers
of the common purple violet (*Viola
odorata*) and of the smaller yellow
violet (*Viola lutea*) are also shown.

Fig. 7. ▷
Fresco detail from the House of the
Golden Bracelet, Pompeii. Typical
fluted bowl fountain set against the
cut, multilobed foliage of an oriental plane tree. The other plants
depicted are, from left to right: a
young oleander, a rose (perhaps
Rosa gallica centifolia), chamomile,
marigold, a strawberry tree, variegated ivy, and a young palm tree.

Fig. 8. △
Fresco depicting Roman country villas set in a pastoral landscape graced with the scattered interventions of man in the form of urns and statues on pedestals, shrines, altars, and "sacred" trees. National Archaeological Museum, Naples.

Fig. 9. ▷
Fresco detail of a typical country shrine erected beside what is perhaps a "sacred" tree. Note the luxuriant growth of vegetation within the balustrade that protects it from grazing herds of sheep and goats. Such picturesque shrines were often imitated in the informal parks of the Romans. National Archaeological Museum, Naples.

B.   Landscape theme frescoes (figs. 8, 9). Murals depicting pastoral landscapes represented not only natural landscape phenomena such as rivers, mountains, woodlands, caves, and springs, but also man's interventions in the natural landscape. Classical villas   many of them romantically ruined—memorial columns, sacred grottoes, and funerary urns imbue these painted landscapes with an antique, arcadian air, which is often enhanced by figures of shepherds tending their flocks. Some painted landscapes were given a more serious and solemn air, with groups of gods and priests gathered around rural altars. This kind of landscape painting became popular, according to Pliny the Elder, during the reign of Augustus (27 B.C.–A.D. 14). In imitation of these paintings, landscaped parks were often created around important Roman villas.

Mosaic pictures, which were usually devised as a means of decorating pavements and floors, survive in many ancient Roman sites and are also useful in helping us to build up an overall picture of the ancient Roman garden (see figs. 131, 146–55). According to Pliny the Elder, mosaics had their origin in Greece, although the first Roman examples date to about 150 B.C. Mosaics consist of small cubes of stone, marble, or glass paste, which were known as *tesserae*. These were bedded in mortar to create patterns, some of which were geometric, others representational. Initially executed in black on a white background (see figs. 28, 71–72), mosaics later became multicolored. Designs often consisted of a central medallion on a figurative theme surrounded by borders featuring geometric or floral repeat patterns. Because of the technique of mosaic, it is often not possible to depict a subject with the precise detail found in fine brush painting. Nonetheless, mosaic pictures excavated at such sites as Carthage and Tabarka in Tunisia feature useful outline depictions of the plants, gardens, and vineyards of Africa in their time.

Horticultural Traditions • Ancient horticultural traditions, some dating back to Roman times, are practiced in parts of Italy today. It is striking, for example, that many of the gardening tools used today seem to be almost exactly the same as those depicted in ancient Roman paintings and mosaics. Terracotta pots currently in use in Italian gardens seem to be very close in shape and size to those used in Roman times. The practice of inserting terracotta pots into house walls to serve as nesting boxes for sparrows, common in old houses in southern Italy, parallels the practice in ancient Rome of inserting such pots into the walls of pools as breeding recesses for fish. Careful observation of traditional horticultural techniques in use today can increase the understanding of similar techniques used in ancient Rome.

GARDEN FUNCTIONS

Roman gardens were developed to serve a variety of functions, chief among which was the provision of outdoor locations for the enjoyment of leisure and the arts, for the promotion and facilitation of health and exercise, and for the production of fruit and vegetables.

Pleasure • Among the principal pleasures of a great Roman villa garden were its elegant pavilions designed for the enjoyment of the arts. Usually set deep in protective vegetation, these pavilions were either square or circular in plan. Some took the architectural form of a temple. Others were surmounted by a roof terrace. Yet others, boasting a number of stories, were in the form of towers. Though they were sometimes linked with each other and with the main villa by covered walks, their location within the garden was chosen so that they would serve as quiet retreats from the bustle of the main villa. Pavilions frequently contained small private theaters, libraries, or museums, and they even had their own small-scale, secluded gardens adjacent to them (see figs. 73, 128). In the gardens of smaller villas, such pavilions were often not of stone but were simple structures of wooden trelliswork shaded by a vine but likewise designed for cultural activities, quiet outdoor dining, and relaxation.

The garden was also a potential stage for displaying works of art, especially sculpture. Collections of antique Greek and Roman statuary were set along a garden's walkways, in garden pavilions, along terraces, or within courtyards.

Mural paintings were prized within small walled gardens. In many cases, the mural paintings on a garden's walls were given as much attention as the frescoes that decorated a villa's interior.

Health and Exercise • Physical health was as important as mental health to the ancient Romans. Many great Roman villa gardens included facilities for private physical exercise: baths, gymnasiums, stadiums, and hippodromes built on a smaller scale than the public facilities enjoyed by the citizens at large. While the ancient Greek gymnasium was a covered colonnade suitably shady for strenuous physical exercise, the colonnades of a Roman gymnasium, particularly a private one, were more frequently used for less strenuous exercises such as walking. The Romans often walked in groups in their gymnasiums, talking and reading aloud to each other so that physical and intellectual exercise were combined. Pliny the Younger wrote that the pleasure of walking in a private gymnasium at his villa at Laurentum was enhanced in spring by the scent of the garden's violets.

Larger villa gardens boasted private stadiums and hippodromes in addition to gymnasiums. Like the gymnasiums, they were used for the gentler exercise of walking, in addition to running and horse-riding exercises. The best-known of these garden facilities is the hippodrome that formed part of the garden at the Tuscan villa of Pliny the Younger, which is described in detail in his writings.

Food Production • A clearer picture of the kitchen gardens attached to Roman villas is emerging from recent archaeological evidence. Excavations in the gardens of villas at Boscoreale, north of Pompeii, have revealed extensive raised vegetable beds. Also found there was a circular wellhead marking the location of a water-storage cistern to supply water for irrigating the vegetable beds. We know that fallowing and crop rotation were used to improve soil fertility and that organic pesticides were in use. A large selection of garden tools was available for cultivation, many of them similar to those used by modern gardeners.

Roman gardens initially contained native species of fruits and vegetables. As the empire spread, new species were introduced from areas with which the Romans had new contact. The techniques of food production were surprisingly advanced. Different methods of soil fertilization and irrigation were used to advantage. Seeds, cuttings, layers, and grafts were all utilized as means of plant reproduction. Various devices were used to protect tender fruit and vegetables and to advance or retard their growth (see fig. 171), and experimental grafting and cross-pollination were carried out to produce fruit with better or different flavors.

GARDEN DESIGN

Two distinct types of Roman gardens can be identified: the enclosed garden, in which buildings entirely or partially surround the garden, and the open garden, which surrounds a building. The enclosed garden is typified by the urban gardens excavated at Pompeii and Herculaneum, the cities submerged by the volcanic eruption of Mount Vesuvius in A.D. 79. The open garden is characteristic of suburban or rural villas, in which views from the garden over the surrounding countryside are possible. This kind of design is exemplified by some of the gardens at the emperor Hadrian's Villa near Tivoli, east of Rome.

Most Roman city gardens were formal in their design, but the gardens of the great Roman villas had distinct areas with different design characteristics. For example, it is well known that the villa at Tivoli contained many garden areas of formal design, but it is less well known that other areas were deliberately landscaped in a contrasting informal style (figs. 10, 11). The park of the emperor Nero (r. A.D. 54–68) within the walls of Rome likewise contained formal areas along with those that were distinctly informal and naturalistic in their design.

Figs. 10, 11.
Hadrian's Villa, Tivoli. Below this circular Temple of Venus was an informal landscape valley that anticipated the English landscape garden familiar in the eighteenth century (see p. 149). The valley was conceived by Hadrian as a representation of the famous Vale of Tempe below Mount Olympus in Thessaly, Greece. The figure of Venus situated on the opposite end of the grass terrace from the temple is a copy of the Cnidian Venus by Praxiteles, the great Greek sculptor.

Formal Gardens • The formal areas of a large garden were usually in the vicinity of a house, their form and proportion tending to follow those of the architecture of the house itself (figs. 12, 13). Occasionally, other, smaller formal gardens would be attached to a subsidiary garden building or pavilion located at a distance from the house within a larger park. Unique to ancient Rome were the formal gardens that were based on the shapes of the great sports arenas of the time. Miniature versions of the characteristic Roman hippodrome, or horse-racing course, were common in gardens. These were usually designed as isolated units within a larger park. They were long, narrow spaces, with the long, straight sides joined by semicircular ends. Examples could be seen at the imperial palace on the Pincian Hill in Rome and at Hadrian's Villa at Tivoli. Some hippodrome-shaped gardens were surrounded by raised gardens echoing the terraced seating that surrounded a real hippodrome.

The culture of ancient Greece was never far from an educated Roman's mind. Some formal gardens were designed with deliberate reference to similar locations in ancient Greece. Cicero describes one of his gardens that had areas named the Lyceum and the Academy in honor of the Greek gardens where the philosophers Aristotle and Plato, respectively, taught. Much later, the emperor Hadrian had areas in his garden similarly named.

The design of the house and garden were so closely linked that vistas designed to run through the house were aligned with the views running through the garden. On occasion, the integrated house and garden vista would stretch from the front door right through the house to terminate at a focal point at the end of the garden. This focal point could take the form of a summer pavilion, a dining alcove, a household shrine, or a grotto or *nymphaeum* (grotto associated with a nymph) erected against the end wall of the garden.

Fig. 12.
Fresco from the House of M. Lucretius Frontus, Pompeii. This painting shows a U-shaped villa enclosing a formal symmetrical garden with an axial approach to the villa's central portico.

Fig. 13.
Frescoes from Pompeii. The exact provenance of these panels, now in the National Archaeological Museum, Naples, is unknown. They depict colonnaded villas with symmetrical facades and formal, symmetrical gardens in front and wooded parks in back.

Informal Gardens • The Romans remained attached to their agrarian origins, and a fondness for naturalism prevailed in Roman culture. It was exemplified in many ways, none more dramatic than the choice of the emperor Tiberius (r. A.D. 14–37) to create an outdoor dining room within a natural sea cave at his Sperlonga villa near Naples (fig. 14). It was also demonstrated in the creation of naturalistic areas in the great villa gardens. Hadrian's Villa at Tivoli contained the area called the Vale of Tempe that was landscaped so as to call to mind the fabled natural beauty of the

Fig. 14.
Sperlonga. The emperor Tiberius had a predilection for building on extraordinary sites. He adapted this natural cave on the coast near Naples as a summer banquet room.

valley of the same name in Greece. Pliny the Younger noted with appreciation his own informal orchard, or "country corner," which contrasted with the overall formal design of his hippodrome garden. Some deliberately informal garden areas were given the aspect of sacred groves (fig. 15). For example, the sanctuary on the Pincian Hill in Rome dedicated to Silvanus, the god of woods and trees, was deliberately rustic in atmosphere in spite of being in the middle of the city.

Many wealthy Romans had hunting parks as part of their country estates. These were kept in as natural a state as possible to provide an ideal habitat for the game being hunted. Deer, boar, fox, and hare were hunted on horseback with hounds, the supply of hares sometimes maintained by warrens—specially reserved areas where the hares could breed in burrows. Depictions of hunting with hounds are found in mosaics from the second and third centuries A.D. that have survived from Carthage and El Djem in present-day Tunisia in North Africa (see fig. 75). Occasionally, North African mosaics also show hunting with falcons.

The Peristyle Garden • City houses usually faced inward to a courtyard, the source of light and air for the rooms arranged around it. These courtyards were sometimes surrounded by a continuous covered colonnade, or peristyle, to provide shelter and shade as well as access from room to room. Such gardens are thus called "peristyle gardens." The earliest peristyle gardens in Pompeii date from the second century B.C., the most magnificent to survive being the garden of the House of the Faun (see figs. 84–85). These gardens are usually, but not always, rectangular in shape. The famous courtyard known as the Maritime Theater at Hadrian's Villa, dating from the second century A.D., is circular.

A colonnade was constructed of freestanding columns arranged at regular intervals around the courtyard and supporting the outer edge of the house roof. Sometimes, low walls or balustrades linked the columns at the bottom.

Occasionally, these low walls between columns were hollowed out on top to provide planting troughs. In the upper space between

much so that in many villas the portico or porticoes came to have a visual importance greater than that of the villa itself. The architectural lines established by the portico were often continued into the design of the garden, becoming the frame around which the garden's paving, pools, and planting beds were developed. Examples can be seen not only at Poppaea's Villa at Oplontis, west of Pompeii (see fig. 104), but also in the frescoes depicting rural and seaside villas that have survived from ancient cities on the Bay of Naples.

The Terrace Garden • On hillside sites, terraces were created in gardens in order to make walking easier but also for the practical reason of soil retention. Each level had its own design, which was usually linked aesthetically with the designs on the other terraces. The late republican terraced gardens of Lucullus and Sallust, located near the Pincian Hill in Rome, have already been mentioned. But terraced gardens are found across the Roman Empire and from many different periods (figs. 17, 18).

A great villa at Stabiae near the Bay of Naples had a garden in which terraces were partly supported by stone or brick vaults. Elaborate architectural staircases linked one level with another. The top and most important terrace was designed around a deep pool. The pool was surrounded by colonnades and shaded by twenty-four magnificent plane trees (*Platanus orientalis*), their crowns rising high above the surrounding roofs.

Fig. 15. ◁
Fresco from the villa of Agrippa Posthumus at Boscotrecase. This painting of an idyllic landscape is now displayed in the National Archaeological Museum, Naples. It shows a cult pillar, or votive column, set on a rocky crag and backed by trees, a kind of landscape ideal that the Romans tried to re-create in their informal parks.

Fig. 16. △
Fresco from villa at Stabiae, near the Bay of Naples, now in the National Archaeological Museum, Naples. Colonnaded waterside villa fronted by a formal terrace and a matching pair of boat piers. Note the semicircular recess on the villa's front, the high viewing tower (or belvedere) attached to the back of the villa, and the background trees, which have been pruned up to form high, close-set foliage canopies.

the columns stretched a metal or wooden pole from which a curtain could be suspended. Pliny the Younger wrote of a red curtain being hung in such a fashion. The curtain could be left open or drawn, depending on how much shade was required in the colonnade.

The Portico Garden • In contrast, rural and maritime villas had colonnades on their exterior, so that the occupants could look out through the columns and enjoy the view over the neighboring land or sea (fig. 16). These external colonnades were similar in their construction and detail to the colonnades within a villa's internal courtyards. Architecturally, the portico acted as a link between the villa's interior and exterior, so

Fig. 17.
Villa Jovis, Capri. On the island of Capri in the Bay of Naples, with its mountainous coastline, high cliffs, and deep caves, the emperor Tiberius developed a series of villas, terrace gardens, and grottoes. Now quite ruined, the sites allow the visitor to mentally reconstruct the scale of the buildings, the diverse terraced levels, and the viewpoints in the gardens.

GARDEN BUILDINGS AND OTHER STRUCTURES

Roman gardens were characterized by the balance achieved between rich and diverse planting on the one hand and strong architectural decoration on the other. Garden architectural elements take many forms, including buildings, pavilions, and other structures.

Altars and Shrines • In general, the Romans were a very religious people. Shrines to the gods were the most precious elements in many family houses and gardens. They were generally dedicated to the Lares, the household gods. Additional shrines were sometimes dedicated to gods and goddesses related to a garden setting. Pliny the Younger described a shrine dedicated to Ceres, the goddess of agriculture and especially corn, in the garden of his villa at Laurentum. Figures of Flora, goddess of flowers; and of Pomona, goddess of fruit and orchards, and Vertumnus, her male counterpart, were used in gardens because of their connections with a garden's activities. It was thought these gods might watch over the crops and protect them.

In large gardens, there was a tendency to place figures of such gods in specially constructed pavilions. In smaller gardens, they were usually placed in a smaller architectural setting such as a niche set in a high garden wall. The niche setting was sometimes given added visual importance with a frame of attached columns or pilasters topped with a pediment. On a table or specially constructed shelf in front of the shrine, offerings of flowers, food, or other gifts would be placed. A small depression was sometimes carved in the top of the table for libations of wine and other liquid offerings (figs. 19, 20).

Fig. 18.
Villa Fersen, Capri. Terraced gardens led out to viewpoints graced by circular belvederes like this one, from which the emperor Tiberius might enjoy distant marine panoramas.

Fig. 19.
Chromolithograph reconstruction of a fresco from the
House of the Amazons, Pompeii. This garden contains
a shrine set in a thicket of laurels and date palms. The
figures in the shrine represent a pair of Egyptian deities.
In the background is depicted a shoreline with three
colonnaded villas.

Fig. 20.
Chromolithograph reconstruction of a fresco from the
House of Sulpicius Rufus, Pompeii. A garden court is
backed by a high hedge of deciduous trees. Within the
court only architectural and sculptural landscape elements are included. Among these are gesturing deities
on plinths, a *pinax* above the gate, and an altar in the
foreground. Offerings and occasional sacrifices were
made on altars such as this.

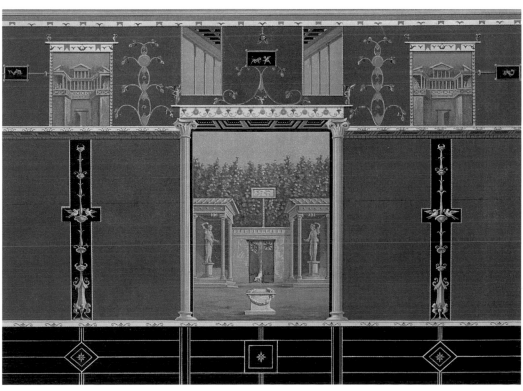

Grottoes and *Nymphaea* • "Grotto" was the name given to a cave, either natural or artificially constructed, that was adapted as a cool summer retreat. Shade was the key ingredient of a successful grotto, since it ensured the desired cool atmosphere. Shade was first provided on the approaches to a grotto. For example, a grotto described by the writer Seneca (ca. 4 B.C.–A.D. 65) at a villa in Cumae, north of the Bay of Naples, was approached through groves of shady plane trees. A plantation of plane trees as well as a crossing over a cooling stream marked the approach to the grotto of Cicero's friend Atticus (ca. 110–32 B.C.). A grotto was preferably oriented away from the sun so that its coolness could be preserved. The two grottoes at Cumae described by Seneca were oriented so that one never received the sun and the other only received a shaft of low sun for a short time before sundown. When the desired northern orientation was not possible, the grotto could be located instead next to a stream or other source of cooling water or by an overhanging tree or group of trees.

Grottoes were sometimes fancifully imagined to be the dwelling places of "nymphs," a class of semidivine beings thought to inhabit woods, hills, rivers, and caves. A grotto so imagined was termed a *nymphaeum*. One of the most famous *nymphaea* of antiquity was that belonging to Atticus. Atticus was much admired for his refined taste. His grotto was known as the Amaltheion, for it was dedicated to Amalthea, a nymph who lived in a cave on Mount Ida in Greece and who, according to Greek legend, was the nurse and savior of the young god Zeus.

City gardens also boasted *nymphaea*, although they were necessarily less rustic in atmosphere and design. The *nymphaeum* at the emperor Domitian's palace on the Palatine Hill in Rome was set in the dark vaults underneath the hillside terraces of its garden. This kind of location was thereafter a popular place in which to make a garden grotto.

Fig. 21.
The House of Neptune and Amphitrite, Herculaneum. The dining alcove in this garden had the *nymphaeum* as its backdrop. Also forming part of the alcove's backdrop was this sumptuous polychrome mosaic representing the deities Neptune and Amphitrite, after whom the house is now named. The rustic decorative theme is reinforced by the flanking wall frescoes depicting gardens and plants.

Fig. 22.
The House of the Grand Fountain, Pompeii. This pedimented fountain is faced with rough tufa stone and shellwork contrasting in texture with the graceful and intricate mosaic of the niche. Water flowed from the open mask in the center and cascaded down the steps to a catchment basin, mimicking water falling in a natural rocky cascade.

Large *nymphaea* were sometimes framed by grand architectural compositions of flanking arcades and niches. In the construction of an artificial grotto, deliberately rough stones were used to simulate the stones of a real cave. Pumice, a form of porous lava, was recommended by Pliny the Elder as being ideal for the purpose. Some *nymphaea* were inset with lions' masks, from whose mouths water spouted into a pool below. *Nymphaea* in small gardens might amount to no more than a niche set into a garden wall. Nonetheless, they would be decorated with pumice and shells in simulation of natural sea caves, and they often featured a trickle of water flowing down over the shells and rocks to make them glisten. Smaller *nymphaea* would sometimes boast a mosaic wall picture based on a marine theme.

The incorporation of water into a *nymphaeum* design was much desired. At the elaborate auditorium of the rich Maecenas (ca. 70–8 B.C.), the friend and patron of the poet Horace (65–8 B.C.), water cascaded down a semicircular flight of steps placed within the *nymphaeum*. A similar thundering cascade was built by Hadrian at Tivoli.

The effect of these cascades was enhanced by the reflected light and the echoing sound that emanated from the nymphaeum interior. At the very least, a *nymphaeum* was expected to have a simple trickle of water representing a natural spring, a favored location for nymphs in the wild (figs. 21–23).

Fig. 23.
The House of the Small Fountain, Pompeii. A small fountain niche against a garden wall gives Its name to a house thought to have belonged to a family of Pompeian fruit merchants. This fountain, like that in the House of the Grand Fountain (fig. 22), is in the form of a pedimented niche covered with mosaic made of vitreous paste and seashells. Water spills from a mask at the center of the niche into a marble-lined basin. Brilliantly colored wall frescoes depicting fantasy landscapes offer illusory extensions of the garden's small space. Today, contemporary bronze figures of a diminutive scale are placed in and on the rim of the basin.

Prospect Towers • Prospect towers, now often called "belvederes," were sometimes built on great estates to allow for a bird's-eye view over the garden and its surrounding landscape (fig. 24; see also fig. 18). Being high, their uppermost rooms caught lofty breezes and served as cool retreats in summer. They were usually attached to the main structure of a villa, but were sometimes built as freestanding structures at some distance from the main building. The belvederes depicted in Roman villa landscape paintings have simple pitched roofs, such as those seen in works from the Boscotrecase site near Naples, but those represented in North African mosaics of the second century have castellated roof lines, indicating perhaps that they also served as watchtowers with a defensive function. Hadrian boasted at least two prospect towers at Tivoli. One was built so that he could enjoy the pleasant prospect up the Vale of Tempe. The other, now called the Roccabruna Tower, was built so that he might look over a nearby river valley. Another emperor who enjoyed a bird's-eye view was Nero, who had a tower within his garden in the city of Rome. From a room on the tower's upper level, he is said to have watched the destruction wrought by the great fire of Rome in A.D. 64. One of Nero's predecessors as emperor, Caligula (r. A.D. 37–41), enjoyed a broad panorama while dining, not in a tower, but in a tree house.

Arbors and Pergolas • Arbors were open garden structures designed to provide comfortable overhead shade to the areas where people sat, dined, and relaxed. Although arbors were sometimes constructed of stone or marble sections, less permanent materials such as brick or timber were also used. The structures were usually furnished with reclining couches. In his *Letters*, Pliny the Younger described an arbor in the garden of his Tuscan villa as a many-windowed retreat shaded by vines with a bed recess inside: "There you can lie and imagine you are in a wood but without the risk of rain." Refreshment for the occupants was sometimes provided by a pool, small fountain, or water cascade, like the one at the House of Loreius Tiburtinus in Pompeii (see figs. 1, 95).

While arbors were designed to shade garden visitors at rest, pergolas were similarly open structures designed to shade walkers as they moved along a garden's pathways. Pergolas were usually constructed with stone or timber pillars at regular intervals along a pathway's side, the pillars supporting a light overhead wooden framework, or lattice, which provided dappled shade for the path below. Grapevines (*Vitis vinifera*), roses (*Rosa* sp.), and gourds (*Cucurbita* sp.) were planted to climb onto the open structure and provide further shade as required. As the superstructure of a pergola was constructed mostly of light, perishable timber, no pergolas have survived in their entirety. However, examples depicted in mural paintings enable us to imagine how they looked. A fresco from a wall in a villa in Pompeii shows a particularly solidly built example (fig. 25).

Fig. 24.
Fresco from the House of the Small Fountain, Pompeii. The streamside belvedere in the form of a two-level structure set on a raised terrace would have provided panoramic views over the surrounding countryside. Note the grove of upright deciduous trees at the rear of the building. National Archaeological Museum, Naples.

Fig. 25.
Fresco from villa at Pompeii. This painting illustrates the use of architectural trelliswork in the Roman garden. Fencing, arbors, corridors, and semicircular recesses are among the many latticework features displayed. National Archaeological Museum, Naples.

Garden Walls • The high boundary walls that enclosed some Roman gardens, especially urban examples, were not seen as merely functional structures. They were also considered opportunities for enhancing a garden's decoration. Garden walls incorporated patterned brickwork, decorative mixtures of brick and stone, and different stones laid in bands of alternating color.

Some garden walls had niches that could be used for statuary. Simpler decorative recesses to house oil lamps for a garden's illumination at night were also used. A small number of walls have been found that boasted elaborate architectural treatments, some with planned schemes of attached columns and pilasters bridged on top by arches or by triangular or semicircular pediments. A fine example can be seen in the garden of the House of Cupid and Psyche in the harbor city of Ostia, near Rome. In some of the gardens excavated at Pompeii, as in those at other sites, the garden walls were used to create illusionistic scenes to make the small space of the garden appear bigger.

Fencing and Balustrades • Roman gardens were often divided into small subsidiary spaces by means of low ornamental fences and balustrades. These low walls and fences were not usually solid but of an open or perforated design, allowing free movement of cooling breezes from one area of the garden to the next. This feature was very desirable during hot summers. The fences were usually constructed of stone or brick, the perforations being in a variety of shapes. Square, diamond, and circular patterns of perforation were frequently used. A popular type of pierced garden wall was that assembled out of U-shaped roof tiles, each course overlapping the one below, resulting in a wall with an interesting fish-scale pattern.

Waist-high wooden lattice fencing was also used as a means of subdividing a garden. This kind of fencing is depicted in many frescoes from Pompeii and Stabiae, near the Bay of Naples. Because of the perishable nature of wood, only fragments of lattice fencing have been found during garden excavations. Nonetheless, the frescoes clearly show a variety of designs. Some depict fencing with regularly inset recesses designed to house such decorative features as flower-filled stone urns, bowl-shaped fountains, or clipped cypress trees (*Cupressus sempervirens*). On occasion, a lattice fence is shown reduced to a minimum height so that it acts merely as an edging to a planting bed. In these cases, reed-woven rather than timber lattice was often used. In other frescoes, a lattice fence is shown constructed above the normal waist height, sometimes at eye level, to provide stronger visual delineation between two garden areas. Occasionally metal rather than wooden lattice is recorded, and in a garden site at Lake Nemi in the Alban Hills near Rome, a luxurious bronze railing has been unearthed.

Balustrades—fences composed of individual stone balusters—also were used to divide distinct spaces in the garden. They were usually constructed of stone or brick. Occasionally, luxury marble balustrades were used. Many of these were decorated on top with rhythmical arrangements of carved finials, busts, vases, or other ornaments. Frescoes often show exotic birds such as peacocks happily perched on top of dividing balustrades or fencing (see fig. 41).

Garden Paths and Drives • The layout of paths in a garden depended on a garden's size. In smaller gardens, there was space for a path to run only from one end to the other, whereas in larger gardens drives and paths usually ran in a circuit around the garden space. Pliny the Younger describes the latter kind of drive at his Laurentum villa (see p. 2). Bordered by a hedge of box (*Buxus sempervirens*) and rosemary (*Rosmarinus officinalis*), it circled a plantation of mulberries (*Morus nigra*) and figs (*Ficus carica*), in the midst of which was located a vine-shaded pergola. Paths such as this were wide enough not only to take parties of pedestrians but also to accommodate

small horse-drawn carriages or litters. Narrower subsidiary paths were used to separate individual planting beds and to provide easy access for maintenance. These paths often had raised edges to reduce the chance that their surfaces would be spoiled by soil spilling over from adjoining beds during digging and cultivation.

Luxury garden paths tended to be paved with stone. Less important paths were finished with sand or with beaten earth. In gardens in outlying areas of the empire, paths are recorded that were finished with finely broken stones, shards of ceramics, and other adaptable waste material. Gravel, because of its free-draining nature, was the surface favored in rainy Britain.

WATER

Water occupied a special place in Roman gardens. During the early period of Roman history, garden pools were filled directly with rainwater from the roofs of adjoining buildings. Later, the roof water was first stored in an underground cistern or in a roof-level holding tank before being redirected to a pool or fountain. Pools in urban gardens were filled with the public water supply from the city aqueducts. For example, Pompeian gardens were able to boast elaborate water features after the construction at the end of the first century B.C. of the aqueduct known as the Aqua Serino. The gardens of country villas had fountains and other water features only if a villa was situated near a natural water source such as a spring, stream, or river. Cicero's villa at Arpinum was fortunately near the confluence of two rivers, and so its garden featured an abundance of water.

Fig. 26.
Cut-stone or cut-marble paving (known as *opus sectile*) inset with a recycled panel of more intricate design. The re-use of old pavement panels in new locations was common. House of the Ephebe, Pompeii.

Pools • Pools in Roman gardens varied in size from the smallest courtyard pools to the large sheets of ornamental water associated with imperial residences or public parks. Some of the latter were designed to be used for large-scale water sports and imperial pageants. Pools also varied in the complexity of their design from the simplest geometric shapes, such as a square or rectangle, to complex groups of interlocking shapes, which were sometimes on different levels and linked to each other by water cascades. Many Roman pools had a distinctive outline derived from recesses around the pool's perimeter. These recesses were often composed as a series of alternating semicircular and rectangular shapes. They provided shady retreats and breeding holes for the fish that were kept in many pools. Considerable aesthetic value was also placed on the reflections that could be enjoyed on the surface of pools and canals (see figs. 2, 64). For example, a sacred

shrine in the House of Diomedes in Pompeii was placed so as to be reflected in a pool.

Pools were usually constructed in concrete, large pools having the concrete poured over wooden piles for extra stability. Associated pipework was fabricated of either wood or lead. Although the inner surface of some Pompeian pools was painted blue, others were lined with tiles, also often blue. Still others had decorative mosaic work, sometimes abstract in design but often representing marine themes with sea gods, dolphins, and other sea creatures (see fig. 74). Luxury pools were lined with marble and dressed stone. Figues 26–29 illustrate the fine colors and details of mosaic work.

Rills, the long artificial canals conceived to mimic natural streams, were sometimes constructed in gardens, as seen in the garden of the House of Loreius Tiburtinus in Pompeii. There water was made to flow down a stepped cascade to

enter a long narrow canal that traversed the garden. A canal on a much larger scale is known to have graced the garden of the consul Agrippa (ca. 63–12 B.C.), in Rome. As already mentioned, some Roman canals were modeled on and named after the Euripus, the narrow natural channel in Greece, through which water flowed first in one direction and then in the other, as the tides rose and fell. It is thought that some hydraulic mechanism may have been in place in these canals to allow the water to flow back and forth in a similar fashion.

Fig. 27.
Pavement in Pompeii of colored mortar inset with white marble *tesserae*, or small marble pieces, arranged to form a large panel with a central star surrounded by a Greek key-pattern frame. The angles are filled with stylized plants and dolphins.

Fig. 28.
Polychrome marble panel in Pompeii framed in a black
and-white mosaic with foliate scrolls and dentil blocks.

Fig. 29.
Column shaft with banded multicolor mosaic decoration
in the National Archaeological Museum, Naples. The geometric lower band is composed of overlapping arcs, while
the upper band has more naturalistic foliate and floral
motifs. The minuteness of the pieces used allows for
exceptional richness of detail.

Fig. 30.
The House of the Ceii, Pompeii. This wide-brimmed stone bowl would have contained water and a small bubbling fountain. The water would have fallen through the mouths of the animal masks that ring the bowl into a recess in the floor below, from which it would have been carried off in an overflow. Note the pedestal elegantly carved with acanthus leaves.

Fountains • Early Roman technology allowed for fountains only in the form of low-level jets of water. These must nonetheless have been attractive, as the bubbling of a low jet imitated that of a small natural spring. Such imitations were at their most effective if jets could be contrived to spurt from some naturalistically designed, moss-covered grotto. A contrasting use of the low-jet fountain was also widespread, with jets bubbling from the surface of water-filled stone bowls or urns (fig. 30). The latter type is depicted in many surviving frescoes.

Advancing technology allowed for more elaborate garden fountains incorporating stone statuary. Figures of gods, goddesses, nymphs, dolphins, fauns, and children were favored. Later still, new fountain technology introduced the use of higher jets to achieve sparkling water and light effects. Through specially angled spigots or nozzles, water could be thrown into pleasant arcs. Such fountains can be seen to great advantage in the excavated gardens of the House of the Water Jets at Conimbriga in present-day Portugal.

Water for fountains was easily accessed if it could be piped, using gravity, from a nearby stream or spring. If the water source was at a lower level than the fountain, a water wheel or water screw could be used to raise it to a holding tank above the fountain level. Fountains were sometimes gravity-fed from a rainwater-filled, high-level storage tank. However, the finite amount of water available from such a tank meant that the fountain could be operated only for a limited time, until the tank ran dry. Such fountains were run only during special festivities. As a further economy, waste water from fountains was often subsequently run out to irrigate the owner's gardens or orchards. Fountains that ran continuously were only possible when they could be supplied with water from the public aqueduct. This was expensive, however, and such fountains became symbols of a garden owner's wealth, not to say extravagance.

Bowl Fountains, Wall Fountains, and Cascades •
Bowl fountains were characteristic ornaments of
a Roman garden. They consisted of water-filled
stone or marble bowls from which a low jet of
water bubbled. Bowls were sometimes fluted and
usually had a broad brim. In Roman paintings,
birds are often depicted standing on these brims
and drinking the water (fig. 31). Some bowls of
the period were raised on bases or on elegant
carved pedestals, and some sported carved stone

handles. Other bowls were positioned above a
shallow depression in a garden's paving that
would catch the fountain's overflow. In many
garden frescoes, bowl fountains were depicted
set in recesses within a line of trellis fencing
(see fig. 31).

Fig. 31.
A pigeon drinks from a fluted fountain bowl set in a recess
of decorative wooden fencing. Faded traces of low, irislike
plants can be seen in the foreground. This fresco, from an
unknown location in Pompeii, is in the collection of the
National Archaeological Museum, Naples. (See also figs.
88, 105 – 6.)

Fig. 32.
Sculpture from the House of Neptune and Amphitrite, Herculaneum, in the collection of the Superintendent of Archaeology, Pompeii. This white marble mask represents an old man of a theatrical or comic aspect, signified by his enlarged mouth, staring eyes, and long beard stylized into six ringlets. An identical mask forms the mouth of a wall fountain in the nymphaeum off the garden of the House of the Small Fountain in Pompeii.

Wall fountains were also characteristic of Roman gardens. These were often in the form of water falling from the mouth of a lion's mask carved in stone and attached to the wall. The water usually fell into a catchment pool provided below. Also used were masks of other wild animals as well as representations of grotesque figures such as Silenus, the drunken old satyr. More elaborate fountains boasted a series of such masks, each spouting water into a common decorative pool or trough (fig. 32).

Artificially constructed waterfalls or stepped cascades, known as water staircases, were also popular (see fig. 22). They were frequently placed against a garden's boundary wall so that water could be conducted down a flight of steps to splash into a pool below. Light sparkled on the white water as it cascaded down, and the sound of the splashing water filled the garden. The steps were usually built of stone, although less expensive examples were constructed in concrete that was then sometimes faced with tiles or mosaic.

A distinctive elaboration on the standard water staircase was a freestanding version. Conceived on a miniaturized scale and usually carved in expensive marble, it was set in the center of an outdoor court or as an important and refreshing ornament in the center of an internal reception room. From an outlet on top of the ornament, water fell down all four sides into a pool set in the floor below.

GARDEN SCULPTURE

Sculpture played an important part in the decoration of Roman gardens. Most large-scale garden sculpture was of stone, but marble, bronze, terracotta, and wood were often used for the smaller figures frequently found in small urban gardens such as those of Pompeii and Herculaneum.

Through the careful choice of sculpture, a garden owner or designer could establish a garden's theme. For example, figures of gods and goddesses could establish a sacred theme. Figures of ancient philosophers would evoke a sense of reflection. Fauns, satyrs, nymphs, or wild animals would conjure up a rustic atmosphere. However, some collections of garden sculpture were appar-

ently without a theme. They might have reflected simply what was available for purchase at the time the garden was being made, or they may have reflected the differing tastes of several generations of the garden owner's family.

The position and arrangement of sculpture in a garden also varied. Some collections of garden sculpture appear to have been placed at random. Others seem to have been placed according to an organized scheme, perhaps related to a building's architecture. For example, a set of sculpted figures might have been placed on pedestals in a garden, one between each of the individual columns of the surrounding peristyle. Alternatively, the figures might have been positioned in front of each column. The writer Athenaeus (flourished ca. A.D. 200) recorded one such arrangement for a pavilion in Alexandria, Egypt, where one hundred statues were each placed in front of a corresponding column of the pavilion's colonnade. Statuary in larger gardens was sometimes placed in a similar way, but in relation to each of an avenue's trees. In some gardens, sculpted figures were positioned to face the house so that they could be enjoyed from the house's rooms. Statues could also be set to face a variety of directions, so that they would be appreciated by someone strolling around the garden.

Religious and Semireligious Sculpture • Records of religious statues in Roman gardens date from a very early period, for the figures were erected in kitchen gardens to act as protectors of the garden's crops. Shrines especially dedicated to the Lares, the protective household gods, were ensured an honored place. A shrine to the Lares is featured in the early garden of the House of the Surgeon at Pompeii.

At a later period, figures of the classical deities, many derived from ancient Greece, were erected in gardens (figs. 33, 34). Deities associated with fecundity, such as Priapus, were favored. Also popular were Ceres, the goddess of corn; Flora, the goddess of flowers; Pomona, who presided over orchards; Vertumnus, her male counterpart; and Silvanus, the god of trees. Venus, a particular protector of gardens and plants, was often represented surrounded by sea nymphs known as

Fig. 33.
Sculpture from the House of Julia Felix, Pompeii, in the National Archaeological Museum, Naples. This white marble statuette belongs to a series of representations of the goddess Venus preparing to bathe. She rests her hand on the head of a small-scale figure of the god Priapus. The group is remarkable for the extensive remains of gilding as well as some traces of paint. The use of small-scale statuettes in addition to larger, human-scale statues is characteristic of the gardens of ancient Rome.

Fig. 34.
Sculpture from the House of Neptune and Amphitrite, Herculaneum, in the collection of the Superintendent of Archaeology, Pompeii. This white marble mask of Pan, one of a pair, was mounted high upon the *nymphaeum* of the house.

Nereids. Cupid, Venus's love child by Mars, was also represented in garden statuary, as were the Egyptian deities Isis and Osiris.

Demigods, such as satyrs, were likewise the subject of garden sculpture. Satyrs were considered appropriate to a garden because they were thought to inhabit forests and woodlands. The Muses, the goddesses who inspired learning and the arts, and nymphs were other popular subjects for garden sculpture. Cicero reflected that statuary figures of the Muses were more appropriate for decorating a writer's garden than were figures of bacchantes, the devotees of Bacchus, the god of wine. During religious festivals, a garden's sacred statuary was often decorated with garlands of flowers and foliage.

Fig. 35.
The Lernaean Hydra, Herculaneum. The malleability of bronze allowed for the creation of finely detailed pieces such as this multiheaded serpent, the mythological Hydra, clinging to the stump of a tree. Serpents are frequently represented in Roman sculpture and painting.

Sculpted figures were sometimes used as hosts on which a gardener might grow and train climbing plants. In a letter to his brother, Cicero described how a gardener had entwined climbing ivy around the fingers of some statuary figures in his garden "so that the figures in a Greek dress appear to be pruning the ivies into shape."

Decorative Sculpture • Garden sculpture did not necessarily have a representational theme. Some was purely ornamental, such as the low-relief carving on the surface of garden vases, bowls, tables, and couches. This carving often comprised abstract motifs of an architectural origin such as a frieze or cornice. In other objects it might feature foliate patterns that were derived from a close observation of leaves and flowers. The most widespread example of the latter was the decorative use of the leaf of the acanthus (*Acanthus mollis*), a plant native to the Mediterranean region. Carved drapery motifs were also used, the folds of a draped cloth represented as abstract patterns. The most distinctive mode of abstract sculpted decoration was what became known as "grotesque." This form of ornament combined motifs derived from animal, vegetable, architectural, and abstract sources and wove them into an integrated whole.

Secular Sculpture • Other garden statuary represented famous rulers, sculptors, philosophers, writers, or characters from well-known dramas of the time. Athletes provided further subjects for sculptors. Among the latter, the two life-size bronze statues of boy athletes found in the garden of the Villa dei Papiri at Herculaneum are perhaps the best known. Playful children were sometimes represented. Their carefree youth and gaiety were thought to reflect the appropriate ambience of an ornamental garden. In some gardens, sculptural figures of wild animals such as boar and deer were introduced to suggest a rural atmosphere. Sculptures of mythological beasts such as griffins were often used as supports for stone garden tables (fig. 35; see also fig. 46).

Fountain Sculpture • The preferred subjects for fountain sculpture in a garden were those associated with water. Figures of river gods, sea nymphs, and Venus with her shell were popular. Also favored were seashells and marine creatures, such as seahorses, sea snakes, and a variety of fish. Dolphins were widely used as sculptural subjects (see fig. 129). Water spurting from the mouths of two or three intertwined dolphin figures was a common fountain theme. Water was made to spill from the mouths of carved dolphin masks mounted on garden walls, and children often were represented riding on a dolphin's back. Figures of children and nymphs were shown spilling water from upturned vessels into a fountain pool (fig. 36). On occasion the association of a fountain figure with water was not so obvious. For example, some fountains were in the form of an enlarged pinecone. In this case the water spilling from its many perforations was thought to put the onlooker in mind of a pinecone spilling its resin.

Fountain figures, especially smaller figures, in bronze were common because the hollow center of a bronze figure could conceal the fountain's pipework. In the case of a stone figure, it was more difficult to conceal water pipes, usually of lead, since the figure had to be bored through to take them. However, even in the latter case, the actual nozzle of the fountain was usually of bronze.

Herms • A particular feature of Roman gardens was the widespread use of a form of garden sculpture known as the "herm." A herm was a stone or bronze bust representing a human head. It was usually placed on top of a short pillar so that it was raised closer to the viewer's eye level (see fig. 171). Frequently, a stone bust and its supporting pillar were carved out of the same piece of stone. These busts were called herms possibly as a variation on "terms," as the figures often were located at the terminus of a walk or vista. The name may also have derived from the possibility that the first examples of these figures represented Hermes.

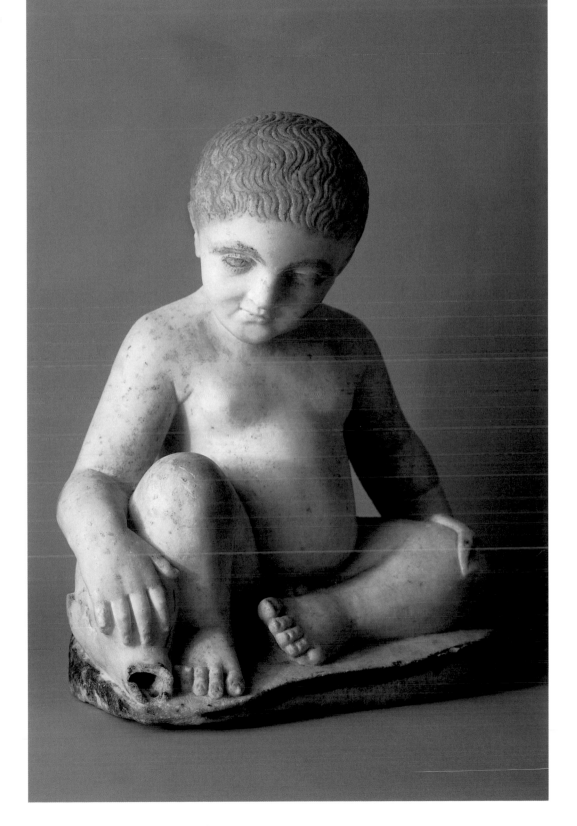

Fig. 36.
Sculpture from the House of the Chaste Lovers, Pompeii. Children were a frequent subject of garden sculpture. They are often depicted as chubby toddlers playfully overturning a water container, as seen here. Such figures often functioned as fountains, with the water outlet in the mouth of the urn. The remains of paint on this figure demonstrate that such figures were frequently painted in realistic colors.

Terminal busts usually represented a god, a demigod, or a famous human. Occasionally they represented racial or national types such as Africans, Berbers, Asians, Germans, or Romanians. Best-known to us are the herms that consisted of two busts carved back to back and sharing the same supporting pillar. The two busts often represented twin aspects of the one figure, such as the male and female, or age and youth. These herms were called janiform because they looked both ways and called to mind Janus, the twin-headed Roman god who guarded doors and entrances.

***Oscilli* and *Pinakes* •** Decorative stone panels sculpted in low relief and sometimes painted were used to decorate gardens. There were two types, the *oscillum* and the *pinax*.

An *oscillum* was a small marble panel carved in low relief both on the front and on the back with a variety of images and motifs. It was light enough to be suspended on a chain from an overhead beam and was frequently hung between the columns of a garden colonnade or a portico, where it would oscillate in a breeze, hence its name. The shape of such a low-relief panel was usually rectangular or round. Some panels were in the shape of a *pelta*, a traditional shield made of animal skin said to have been used by the mythical female warriors known as Amazons. Occasionally, an *oscillum* took the form of a stone mask (figs. 37–40).

Although *pinax* could refer to a flat painted panel, many *pinakes* in Roman gardens were also in low relief. A *pinax* was decorated on the front and back and of similar shapes to those of an *oscillum*. Instead of being suspended from above on a chain, however, a *pinax* was displayed mounted on a stone shaft (fig. 41).

Fig. 37.
Oscillum from the House of the Citharist, Pompeii, in the collection of the Superintendent of Archaeology, Pompeii. In this low-relief carving a hunter with bow and arrow and hounds kills a stag emerging from a forest. It is thought this subject may refer to one of the Labors of Hercules. The crescent shape of this *oscillum* is based on the *pelta*, the traditional shield made of animal pelts.

Fig. 38.
Oscillum from the House of the Relief of Telephus, Herculaneum, in the collection of the Superintendent of Archaeology, Pompeii. Low-relief figure of a dancing maenad, her gracefully curving arms upholding an enveloping mantle.

Fig. 39.
Oscillum from the House of the Relief of Telephus, Herculaneum, in the collection of the Superintendent of Archaeology, Pompeii. Bearded figure of Pan carrying a flaming torch and covered basket as he approaches a blazing altar.

Fig. 40.
The House of the Relief of Telephus, Herculaneum. Some of the *oscilli* at this site have been reinstalled, suspended between the columns of the atrium. Note the central water basin with integral planting troughs.

Fig. 41.
Fresco depicting a dove perched on a *pinax* and a peacock on a typical trellis fence. National Archaeological Museum, Naples.

Fig. 42.
Sundial from the Temple of Apollo, Pompeii. This dial with a hemispherical face sits atop an Ionic column. About thirty sundials of different forms have been recovered in Pompeii. Some have hemispherical faces, others have flat or conical faces. In some the dial is vertical, in others horizontal.

Sundials • Sundials were usually carved on a panel of stone that was then erected either high on a freestanding pillar or on the wall of a sunny courtyard. An example of a sundial on a pillar can be found in the courtyard of the Temple of Apollo in Pompeii (fig. 42). Although dials have often been found in the gardens of small houses, the most famous one was that in the public park near the Mausoleum of Augustus in Rome. There a large horizontal sundial was inscribed in the park's paving. To provide a suitably large gnomon —the marker whose shadow indicates the correct time on a dial—a granite obelisk was imported from Egypt.

GARDEN FURNITURE

Outdoor relaxation and dining were part of summer life in an ancient Roman garden. This created the need for a variety of garden furniture, some of which was built in as part of the garden architecture. For example, built-in masonry couches were an important feature for outdoor meals, as Romans usually ate while reclining rather than sitting. Fabric cushions, covers, and other textiles made the couches comfortable when they were in use. The dining couches were usually arranged around three sides of a central serving table, in an arrangement called a "triclinium." The fourth side was left free to allow access to the table or tables. Although couches were occasionally carved in marble or stone, they were usually cast in concrete, which was sometimes covered with decorative mosaics or paintings (figs. 43, 44).

Fig. 43.
Dining room recently excavated at Murecine, near the Bay of Naples. A dining alcove, whether indoors or outdoors, was often planned in the form of a triclinium, in which three built-in masonry couches — Romans dined while reclining rather than sitting — formed three sides of the alcove's square. The fourth side was left open to allow for service. A circular table in the alcove center had a water outlet with which to wash or cool the food before serving.

Fig. 44.
Couch in dining room at Murecine. A detail illustrates how the surface of each couch in a triclinium sloped upward toward the alcove's center and had a pillow-like headpiece and a narrow shelf incorporated along the front for resting drinking and other vessels. Cushions and coverlets made the couches comfortable.

Fig. 45.
Table pedestal (side view) from the House of the Prince of Naples, Pompeii, in the collection of the Superintendent of Archaeology, Pompeii. The side view of this pedestal shows its vigorous three-dimensional modeling. The figure of Silenus emerges from an acanthus leaf that in turn emerges from the upper part of a lion's leg.

Fig. 46.
Table support from the House of Cornelius Rufus, Pompeii, in the collection of the Superintendent of Archaeology, Pompeii. This white marble table support is carved from a white marble slab. The support is luxuriously carved in the form of a pair of mythical creatures with lions' masks and paws, rams' horns, and wings that combine features from sphinxes and griffins. The creatures frame low-relief carvings representing tufts of stylized twining foliage.

Garden tables in stone or marble usually had simple rectangular tops. They were supported on pairs of decorative stone panels, which were often carved in low relief with representations of mythical or fantastical beasts. Winged griffins or lions were the beasts most favored. These animals also were used to decorate the legs of circular three-legged tables, which have been found in excavations (figs. 45–47). Archaeological evidence suggests that, in addition to this fixed furniture, use was made of light movable furniture constructed of wood or of basketwork.

Fig. 47.
Table from the House of the Golden Cupids, Pompeii, in the collection of the Superintendent of Archaeology, Pompeii. This marble occasional table with a circular top features a white marble pedestal carved in imitation of a rustic wooden club. The knots in the "wooden" trunk are realistically depicted.

PLANTING

Despite the wealth of architectural and sculptural ornaments in their gardens, the Romans never lost sight of the fact that the true object of a garden was to display the joys of nature as seen in its plants. Roman garden planting was characterized by the use of many native evergreen trees and shrubs: pine (*Pinus pinea*), bay laurel (*Laurus nobilis*), laurustinus (*Viburnum tinus*), arbutus (*Arbutus unedo*), myrtle (*Myrtus communis*), box (*Buxus sempervirens*), and ivy (*Hedera* sp.), for example. However, plants imported from other regions were prized also. The use of exotic plants in gardening is a tradition going back beyond Roman times to ancient Mesopotamia, at least. For example, Assyrian records mention exotic trees as part of the plunder available from the conquest of foreign lands. Later, Egyptian gardens also contained many exotics, probably because the Nile Delta itself contains few native plant species. The Romans followed in this tradition, importing garden plants from the many countries they interacted with through conquest or trade.

The plants chosen for a Roman garden depended very much on the climate, on whether the garden was located along the dry Mediterranean coastline, inland in the cooler mountains, or in the northern parts of the empire in central and western Europe. However, even in hot North African gardens, where water for irrigation was scarce, a rich range of plants was grown.

The fresco paintings that survive offer an excellent guide to the arrangement of plants in Roman gardens. The paintings usually show tiered planting, in which small plants are in the front of a bed or border, shrubs are in the middle ground, and trees are in the background. Some frescoes show that mixed plantings were punctuated rhythmically by solitary evergreen cypresses. Although frescoes show very dense plantings, archaeological evidence suggests that garden plants were, in fact, much more widely spaced than is shown in these paintings.

In some gardens, plants were chosen to suggest a specific natural landscape setting. For example, a planting of meadow flowers would be designed to suggest an open plain in one part

of a garden while shade- and water-loving plants would conjure up the environment of a stream-filled defile in another part of the garden. Garden plants were chosen also for their association with one god or another. In his *Natural History*, Pliny the Elder confirms "that different trees are kept perpetually dedicated to their own divinities, the winter-oak to Jove, the bay to Apollo, the olive [*Olea europaea*] to Minerva, the myrtle to Venus, the poplar to Hercules." (The winter-oak is presumably the evergreen oak [*Quercus ilex*].) As the white poplar (*Populus alba*) was associated with Hercules, its leaves were used as his emblem. Ivy's heart-shaped leaves were one of the symbols of Bacchus. The hyacinth (*Hyacinthus orientalis*) as well as the bay tree belonged to Apollo. As Virgil (70–19 B.C.) wrote in one of his *Eclogues*, "My garden is Apollo's seat; I give him gifts of the bay tree and the hyacinth."

The most sophisticated Roman gardens boasted an aesthetic unity between a garden's planting and its architecture and sculptural decoration. For example, formal garden planting often closely followed the architectural lines of a house or villa. Trees were sometimes planted in lines to echo the rhythms of columnar porticoes. Architectural symmetry was often reflected in a garden's plantings. In the garden of the House of the Chaste Virgins in Pompeii, a walk was flanked by symmetrical plantings of alternating roses and junipers (*Juniperus communis*).

The description by Pliny the Younger of the "hippodrome" in his Tuscan garden contains one of the most detailed accounts we have of the planting of a Roman garden. He describes how this area of his garden was surrounded by oriental plane trees that were trimmed upward so that their clear trunks formed a vegetable "colonnade." Ivy was trained in swags so that it hung from tree to tree. In addition, box was planted between each plane tree. Outside the lines of trees, plantings of bay laurel provided a surrounding evergreen screen. At either end of the long lines of plane trees were shady walks through semicircular groves of cypress (presumably tall columnar Italian cypress) and topiaries mainly in the form of "figures" (representations of human or animal forms) and "names" (words formed along the ground from clipped box or other plantings). There were also lawns with fruit trees. The interior of the hippodrome space was planted with two rows of smaller plane trees, with liberally scattered clumps of acanthus and more topiary "figures" and "names." Between the plantings in this interior space, the ground was covered with a carefully dressed topping of clay or sand. Finally, Pliny describes a white marble dining table located at one end of the garden. It was shaded overhead by trelliswork supported on four columns of matching white marble.

Trees • The creation of shade is the first task of a gardener in the hot Mediterranean climate. So numerous were the tree- and vine-shaded courtyards in Pompeii that an observer looking down from above would have seen a "green" city. Native trees such as the sweet chestnut (*Castanea sativa*), the Italian cypress, the stone pine, and the Aleppo pine (*Pinus halepensis*) grew in abundance, as did tall native shrubs such as laurel and oleander (*Nerium oleander*). Other native trees were used occasionally, as referenced by ancient writers. Virgil, for example, mentioned limes (or lindens [*Tilia* sp.]) and elms (*Ulmus campestris*). Horace referred to the white poplar as a garden tree. Pliny the Elder recommended planting the nettle tree (*Celtis australis*) for its elegant bark and edible fruits.

Fig. 48.
Fresco detail from the House of the Golden Bracelet, Pompeii. Valuable information on the planting in a Roman garden is provided in this painting. Depicted against a background of oleander foliage are, from left to right: Madonna lilies (*Lilium candidum*), opium poppies, a chamomile with its daisylike flowers, a twining white-flowered morning glory (*Ipomoea* sp.), and a rose, perhaps *Rosa gallica centifolia*.

The oriental plane tree, which had been used to shade the urban squares of ancient Greece, was imported to Italy by sophisticated Romans who were adherents of classical Greek culture. It was perhaps the most widely used tree for ornamental planting. Pliny described a small internal courtyard at his Tuscan villa that was shaded by four symmetrically planted planes. The plane tree was adaptable and could be planted successfully not only in small private gardens but also in very large ones. The poet Martial (A.D. ca. 40–ca. 104) praised the oriental plane for the planting of avenues, which the architectural writer Vitruvius (first century B.C.) stated should play a part in every gentleman's country estate. Other exotic trees were planted as well. The date palm (*Phoenix dactylifera*), imported from the Near East, was frequently depicted in garden frescoes.

Fruit trees were used to shade the small gardens and courtyards of Pompeii. For example, the remains of fig, cherry, and olive trees (*Olea europaea*) have been found in the garden of the House of Julius Polybius. At a nearby garden in Oplontis, a double row of citron trees (*Citrus medica*) was found, each planted in alignment with a column from the villa's portico.

Tree planting varied in the formality of its arrangement. Although excavations at Pompeii have revealed garden courts in which trees appear to have been planted at random, in other courts, a large fruit or nut tree was formally placed in the center and/or at each corner of the court. Excavations have revealed, for example, a sweet chestnut tree planted at the center of one of the courtyards of a villa at Oplontis.

Shrubs • The most commonly depicted shrubs in garden frescoes are the native evergreen shrubs such as laurel, myrtle, oleander, laurustinus, and bay laurel. (The latter appears to have been grown in a variegated form and in a pale-leafed form as well as in the normal green-leafed form.) Roses are less commonly depicted, but there are a number of literary references to them. For example, Martial boasted that some of his garden roses were what we today call "repeat flowerers," producing two flowerings a year. Among dwarf shrubs used for ornamental landscaping, the evergreen butcher's broom (*Ruscus aculeata*) was recommended by Pliny the Elder. Rosemary was also used and was particularly recommended for seaside gardens like that of Pliny the Younger at Laurentum.

Climbing Plants • The Romans took a keen interest in climbing plants because they could provide shade if they were grown on a garden's colonnades, walls, or trellis screens. The grapevine (*Vitis vinifera*) and the morning glory (*Ipomoea* sp.) were the climbing plants most frequently used. Evergreen smilax (*Smilax aspera*) and ivy were popular as well, and melons (*Cucumis melo*) and cucumbers (*Cucumis sativus*) were trained to scramble on low fences and balustrades. Climbing plants could be trained in the form of decorative swags, which were suspended on ropes between the columns of a colonnade and sometimes between the trunks of regularly spaced trees.

Archaeological evidence has revealed the way in which climbing plants were grown and trained. Climbing plants often were grown from terracotta pots set underground. Excavations have shown that these pots were tilted ingeniously in the direction in which the climbing plant was meant to grow. If it was intended that a plant was to be trained to a column, then its pot would have been set underground slightly tilted in the direction of the column. Other archaeological evidence has uncovered the nail holes in garden walls that were used in the support of plants climbing on the wall.

Flowers • Although trees and shrubs predominated in Roman gardens, flowers, particularly native species, were common (figs. 48, 49). The martagon lily (*Lilium martagon*), Madonna lily (*Lilium candidum*), wild chrysanthemum (*Chrysanthemum* sp.), poppy (*Papaver rhoeas*), and periwinkle (*Vinca minor*) are all shown in garden frescoes. The iris (*Iris* sp.), laurel rose (*Cistus laurifolius*), and daisy (*Bellis perennis*) are depicted in a mural now in the Terme Museum in Rome. Recent excavations in garden soils at Pompeii and neighboring sites have produced seeds of flowers such as asters (*Aster* sp.), pinks (*Dianthus* sp.), mallows (*Malva* sp.), campanulas (*Campanula* sp.), lychnis (*Lychnis* sp.), chickweed (*Cerastium* sp.), and plantains (*Plantago major*).

Fig. 49.
Fresco detail from the House of the Golden Bracelet, Pompeii (see fig. 4). A warbler is shown perched on a hollow-stemmed bamboo (possibly *Arundo donax*). The bamboo is being used to support a shrub rose with carmine-colored double flowers, probably a form of *Rosa gallica centifolia*; the daisy-like flowers are thought to be feverfew (*Chrysanthemum parthenium*) and the larger colored flowers to be the Caen anemone (*Anemone coronaria*); all are southern European natives. As these plants flower in different seasons, the painter has taken artistic license in depicting them in flower together. However, the accuracy and detail with which the plants are represented are akin to those normally associated with botanical illustration.

Literary sources give us further information about the flowers that were grown in gardens. Virgil referred to violets (*Viola* sp.), narcissi (*Narcissus* sp.), hyacinths, vervain (*Verbena officinalis*), and poppies. Pliny the Elder recommended planting hound's-tongue (*Cynoglossum officinale*), with blue borage-like flowers, in combination with blue forget-me-nots (*Myosotis* sp.) for parterres. He also recommended planting the pale yellow kidney vetch (*Anthyllis vulneraria*). Pliny the Younger praised the acanthus for its glossy, undulate foliage. All of these flowers and plants were native to Italy.

As a consequence of the expansion of the Roman Empire from the first century A.D. onward, many new plants were imported, resulting in a tremendous increase in the range of plants available for gardens. Notable among them were those imported from Greece, which included not only Greek natives but also exotic families that had been grown in Greece for a very long period. These included the many plants obtained by the Greeks after their capture of Persia in the fourth century B.C. In turn, such plants would have included not only examples native to the Near East but also examples from the Far East, such as those of the citrus family, which had been obtained by the Persians through their ancient diplomatic and trading ties with China and other countries in the region.

Ferns and Bulbs • At least two fern species were grown as ornamental plants in Roman gardens: the hart's-tongue fern (*Phyllitis scolopendrium*) and the maidenhair fern (*Adiantum pedatum*). The hart's-tongue fern is depicted at the front of mixed borders in some garden frescoes. The maidenhair fern, a plant that grows naturally in shady rock crevices, was frequently planted among the stones of garden grottoes.

Although it is reasonable to assume that many bulbs native to Italy—such as crocus (*Crocus* sp.), gladiolus (*Gladiolus* sp.), allium (*Allium* sp.), and scilla (*Scilla* sp.)—were grown in gardens, the narcissus, also a native, is the only one shown in garden paintings. On the other hand, irises, although strictly speaking rhizomes rather than bulbs, are frequently depicted.

Fruits, Vegetables, and Other Food Plants • The production of vegetables and fruits in kitchen gardens was a highly developed skill for centuries before Roman times. Walled gardens with pears (*Pyrus communis*) and with vegetables such as leeks (*Allium ampeloprasum*) are evidenced from the Mycenaean Bronze Age in Greece. Literary evidence of vegetables in Roman gardens includes the encyclopedist Cato's references to the cabbage family (*Brassica* sp.) and to asparagus (*Asparagus officinalis*) and Pliny the Elder's notes on fennel (*Foeniculum vulgare*), parsnip (*Pastinaca sativa*), mustard (*Brassica negra*), and samphire (*Crithmum maritinum*). We also know the names of many vegetables and herbs introduced by the Romans to colonies such as Britain: celery (*Apium graveolens*), coriander (*Coriandrum sativum*), cucumber, dill (*Anethum graveolens*), fennel, garlic (*Allium sativum*), mustard, onion (*Allium cepa*), orache (*Atriplex hortensis*), parsley (*Petroselinum crispum*), radish (*Raphanus sativa*), and turnip (*Brassica campestris*).

Flowers were also grown in kitchen gardens for their decorative value. A Virgilian tale offers a description of a kitchen garden bordered with white (Madonna) lilies, vervain, hyacinths, and poppies. (Poppies were not only decorative but also useful for their seeds, which had been used in bread making, it is conjectured, as far back as the sixth century B.C.)

In gardens located in the hot Mediterranean climate, rows of vegetables were often grown in the shade of fruit trees.

Of fruit trees depicted in garden frescoes, the quince (*Cydonia oblonga*) and the pomegranate (*Punica granatum*) are the most common. Both golden plums (*Prunus italica*) and purple ones (*Prunus domestica*) are also shown (figs. 50–54). Literary sources reveal the cultivation of an even wider range of fruits. Pliny the Elder lists apples (*Malus* sp.), pears, grapes, cornels (*Cornus mas*), medlars (*Mespilus germanica*), mulberries, service-berries (*Sorbus domestica*), and carobs (*Ceratonia siliqua*) as edible fruits. He also writes of lemons (*Citrus limon*), and we know that oranges (*Citrus aurantium*), natives of the Far East, fruited in some imperial gardens. The Romans introduced to Britain many fruit trees, such as almond (*Prunus dulcis*), apricot (*Prunus armeniaca*), bullace (*Prunus domestica*), medlar, mulberry, fig, grape, pear, plum,

Fig. 50.
Fresco detail from the Villa of Poppaea, Oplontis. This painting shows a twin-handled glass bowl filled with ripening fruit.

Fig. 51.
Fresco detail from the Villa of Poppaea, Oplontis. A decoratively woven willow basket holds figs (*Ficus* sp.) in green and black varieties. Pliny described twenty-nine different varieties being grown in his day.

and quince as well as nut trees such as sweet chestnut and walnut (*Juglans regia*). The wider distribution of plants was one of the boons resulting from the expansion of the Roman Empire.

Many of the fruit species grown in Rome had been imported to the region from abroad. Examples included cherry, brought from the Pontic region of present-day Turkey; the apricot from Armenia; the peach (*Prunus persica*) and the damson plum (*Prunus damascena*) from Syria; and the pomegranate and the jujube (*Zizyphus jujube*) from North Africa. Unusual varieties of more common fruits such as apples were also imported: a "round apple" variety from western Greece, a "Syrian red" variety, as well as a variety without seeds from Belgium. In addition, new apple and pear varieties were bred and selected at home. These new varieties were often given the names of the agricultural estates where they had been produced, such as the Scadian apple and the Dolabellian pear. The technique of grafting fruit trees was quite advanced. Fruit trees with two or three varieties grafted onto one trunk were favored. In *Natural History*, Pliny the Elder mentions a famous tree at Tivoli that had "nuts on one branch, berries on another, while from other places hung grapes, pears, figs, pomegranates, and various sorts of apple." Native fruit species such as wild strawberry (*Fragaria vesica*), raspberry (*Rubus idaeus*), blackberry (*Rubus* sp.), and crab apple (*Malus sylvestris*) were cultivated as well.

Fig. 52.
Fresco detail from the House of the Orchard, Pompeii. The lemon (*Citrus limon*) and its variant, the citron (*Citrus medica*), natives of Persia, were introduced to Roman gardens via the Near East and North Africa.

Fig. 53.
Fresco detail from the House of Julia Felix, Pompeii, in the National Archaeological Museum, Naples. Grapes (*Vitis vinifera*), pomegranates (*Punica granatum*), figs (*Ficus carica*), and apples (*Malus* sp.), among other fruit, fill a glass bowl. Vines were important in Roman life, and many varieties were known for both eating and drinking. They were multipurpose plants in gardens, providing grapes for the table and for winemaking as well as shade for bowers and pergolas.

Potted Plants • The discovery of terracotta pots in considerable numbers during recent garden excavations has led to a better appreciation of their widespread use in the Roman garden. The discovery of both whole pots and pots that had been deliberately smashed has led us to realize that pots were used in two ways. For one, they were used conventionally to hold plants growing above the ground. The agricultural writer Palladius recommended planting pomegranates in large terracotta pots, and Pliny the Elder suggested that lemon trees should be grown in pots. This practice facilitated root pruning for better fruit production. In the second kind of use, plants were transferred from a nursery to the place of planting in terracotta pots. During the process of planting, these pots were deliberately smashed to allow the roots of the plants to spread out from the pot and expand freely into the surrounding soil.

Potted plants were sometimes set out methodically as part of a decorative garden scheme. In the palace garden of King Herod the Great at Jericho (ca. 15 B.C.), in present-day Jordan, there was a great niche, or recess, with tiers of stone steps thickly set with potted plants that were rotated to create a constantly changing "theater" of flowers and foliage.

Fig. 54.
Fresco from the House of M. Lucretius Frontus, Pompeii. This frieze depicts peaches (*Prunus persica*) (or perhaps plums?), figs, garlic (*Allium sativum*), and almonds (*Prunus dulcis*), all of which were cultivated in Roman gardens. However, dates (*Phoenix dactylifera*), which are also shown, are difficult to grow in Italy and so may have been imported from the Near East.

Plants for Garlands • An aspect of Roman planting that is sometimes neglected is the growing of plants for making garlands, wreaths, and crowns, which formed an important element in Roman festivities and celebrations. What plants were favored for this purpose? Horace recommended myrtle and "pliant" parsley. Athenaeus favored decorative larkspur (*Delphinium* sp.), lily, narcissus, and rose. Many varieties of roses were grown for garlands as well as for ornamentals in the garden. Among those known to us are the Rose of Paestum (*Rosa x damascena "Bifera"*), which bloomed twice a year; the Rose of Praeneste (possibly *Rosa gallica*), which was known as a late-flowering variety; and the Rose of Cyrene (possibly *Rosa sempervirens*), about which we know only that it was a native of present-day Libya. Also grown were two native wild rose species, whose descriptions correspond to the roses we know today as *Rosa bifera* and *Rosa gallica centifolia*. The latter was possibly the "cabbage"-type rose referred to by Pliny the Elder.

Topiary and Hedges • The range of trees and shrubs available to a gardener in ancient Rome was limited by today's standards. Therefore, creating topiaries, or plants trimmed into decorative shapes, added to the variety of interesting forms in a garden. Topiaries were especially attractive in a small garden, as they allowed the owner to have trees, such as the cypress, normally associated with a larger garden but in a trimmed miniaturized form.

In his *Natural History*, Pliny the Elder described topiary as the art of sculpting plants into predetermined representational shapes. He credits its inception to C. Mattius, a friend of the emperor Augustus. The first specific topiary recorded was in a letter of Cicero's from 54 B.C. that described having seen evergreen topiaries, one of them sculpted to represent a fleet of ships and another to represent a hunting scene. Pliny wrote that topiary representing specific characters and scenes decorated many of Rome's public spaces. In addition to representational forms, geometric shapes were popular. These included architectural forms such as arches, obelisks, arcades, niches, and pediments.

As for hedges, cypress was used for tall, wall-like divisions within the garden, whereas box was used for lower hedges (see figs. 161, 181, 182). We know that the box hedges in the garden of Pliny the Younger were trimmed not in one low level but in tiers.

Fig. 55. △
Fresco detail from the House of Menander, Pompeii.
An Egyptian gallinule steps through native flowers
thought to be rocket (*Hesperis matronalis*), flax (*Linum*
sp.), and fenugreek (*Taigonella foenum-graecum*). These
flowers are depicted with artistic license rather than with
botanical correctness.

Fig. 56. ◁
Fresco detail from the House of the Labyrinth, Pompeii.
Turtle doves, noted for their affection toward their mates,
are shown perched on a curtain rod. These attractive birds
were popular as pets. Curtains were often suspended in
gardens and porticoes to provide shade.

Fig. 57. ▷
Fresco detail from the Temple of Isis, Pompeii. Egyptian
ibis with a stalk of grain in its beak and a coronet whimsi-
cally placed on its head.

GARDEN FAUNA: BIRDS, ANIMALS, AND FISH

Frescoes reveal that the bird population in Roman
gardens must have been abundant (figs. 55–59).
Doves, pigeons, blackbirds, thrushes, yellow orioles, goldfinches, flycatchers, nightingales, bunt-
ings, and warblers have all been identified in
depictions. In other murals, larger birds such as
peacocks, pheasants, partridges, herons, ibises, and
golden orioles are shown roaming freely through
gardens. We know from literary sources that tamed
birds such as starlings and magpies were also common. Their wings must have been pinioned to
prevent them from flying away.

In addition to these free-ranging birds, birds
in aviaries were popular. The earliest aviaries were
formed by hanging hemp nets across the front
of wall recesses. Freestanding aviaries were more
usual later. Parrots and ornamental ducks in an
aviary are depicted in a garden mural at the
House of Livia on the Palatine Hill. We also know
that Lucullus, the famous epicure, had a dining
room created within an aviary at his villa so that
his guests could have the curious enjoyment of
eating cooked fowl while being surrounded by
their still-alive "cousins."

Fig. 58.
Fresco detail from Herculaneum. A warbler pauses in a field with daisies (*Bellis perennis*). National Archaeological Museum, Naples.

Fig. 59.
Fresco detail of peacocks on ornamental bronze perches. National Archaeological Museum, Naples.

Smaller birds were housed in portable cages usually made of wood or wicker, though metal ones are also recorded. The poet Statius (A.D. ca. 45–96) documented a luxury parrot cage made of silver and ivory. These cages were made in various forms, but those of a circular domed construction were the most elegant.

Large town houses had pigeon houses, or dovecotes, to provide table fowl. There is one, for example, in the garden of the House of the Faun at Pompeii, and Martial wrote of the white dovecote in his garden. Rural villas also had dovecotes, which were either freestanding or incorporated into one of the villa's towers. A dovecote provided a year-round source of protein in the form of meat and eggs, as well as droppings, which were useful as fertilizer. Duck ponds were featured at some country villas.

Rural villas sometimes boasted exotic wild animals such as lions, which were kept for display in menageries (see fig. 148). Native animals were allowed to roam freely in walled hunting parks. The agricultural writer Varro described dining on a raised platform in his hunting park while a bugler used his music to entice deer, boar, and other animals from the forest. In *On Rural Affairs*, Varro reported how he encouraged wild animals to enter his garden occasionally. This he felt was a necessary corrective to the otherwise over-refined nature of his garden.

Although honey was derived mostly from wild bees living in the woods and on the heaths, domesticated swarms were encouraged in gardens through the cultivation of thyme (*Thymus* sp.) and other nectar-rich plants.

Fish were kept in many gardens. Fishponds or pools were characterized by their indented perimeters, which provided shady nooks for fish in hot weather. Amphorae, or wine storage vessels, were sometimes built into pool walls to provide holes in which the fish might breed. Licinius Murena the Elder (first century B.C.) is credited with revolutionizing the technique of breeding fish in captivity. Eventually quite complex pools were being designed, with several interconnecting basins and distinct compartments so as to separate incompatible fish from one another. Varro refers to an arrangement whereby some pools or parts of pools were filled with seawater for the maintenance of seawater fish, while others contained freshwater for freshwater fish. In spite of these complex arrangements, written records are disappointing, confirming only two fish species kept in this way: mullet and sea eel.

CONCLUSION

Until recently archaeologists and art historians have concentrated their study on the architectural remains and artifacts of ancient Roman civilization. More recent studies have focused on the garden history of the period, but with a concentration on the architectural and artistic aspects of the garden. The study of Roman gardens is being taken further at the present time by the analysis of plant remains in the garden soils (see Suggestions for Further Reading, p. 165). Thus, for the first time, a complete picture of the gardens of ancient Rome, in all their complexity, is emerging.

II

FROM IMPERIAL PALACES TO PUBLIC PARKS: THE ROMAN GARDENING WORLD

ROMAN GARDENS can be divided into a number of different types. Most significant in terms of size and sophistication were the gardens of the emperors, which fell into two categories: the imperial palace gardens, located in an urban setting, and the imperial villa gardens, attached to the country estates that served as the emperors' retreats. Of equal interest are the city and villa, or country, gardens that belonged to the Roman elite. Historians have focused less on the sacred groves, public parks, and market gardens of classical Rome; these less domestic landscapes nonetheless formed an important component of the Roman gardening world.

The House of the Marine Venus, Pompeii. See fig. 86.

IMPERIAL PALACE GARDENS

The Palatine Hill in Rome was the location of the official imperial residence from the time of the first emperor, Augustus (r. 27 B.C.–A.D. 14). Some of the other early emperors preferred to live in different parts of Rome, but after the end of Domitian's reign in A.D. 96, the Palatine Hill was occupied for more than three hundred years by the reigning emperors. As succeeding rulers rebuilt old palaces in addition to building new ones, their gardens underwent many transformations. Emperors and their wives adapted the gardens for their own particular uses or updated them to conform to the latest styles and techniques. With a few exceptions, the imperial palace gardens were elaborate ornamental courtyard gardens graced with pools, fountains, and mosaics. Not much of them remains because their Palatine site was adapted in the sixteenth century by Cardinal Alessandro Farnese for his own gardens (the Orti Farnesiana, which were famous in their day)

The Early Emperors • Augustus displayed great personal modesty. His house was not a palace but a simpler dwelling of a type typical of the aristocracy of his day. There is no evidence of a large garden around his house, but we do know that the Roman senate planted a laurel, the symbol of the god Apollo, on either side of Augustus's front entrance in tribute to the emperor.

Augustus did begin to install official gardens on the hill about 20 B.C., including a sacred grove in which stone memorials and shrines were placed informally under the trees. There was a particularly sunny area in the garden that was known as "Syracuse" because the spot put the imperial family and its visitors in mind of the city of that name in sunny Sicily.

Augustus's successor, Tiberius (r. A.D. 14–37), displayed a taste for riches and splendor in the luxurious palace he built on the Palatine Hill, whose rooms were grouped around a courtyard. Perhaps it was as splendid as the many subsequent great courtyard gardens to be laid out on the hill, but little remains due to centuries of building and rebuilding on the site. The interest of the later emperor Claudius (r. A.D. 41–54) in the imperial gardens is not known, but it is recorded that his wife, Messalina, so coveted the famous Roman garden built in the previous century by Lucullus that its owner was forced to commit suicide so that she could take possession.

Nero (r. A.D. 54–68) • Nero chose not to live in the traditional palace complex on the Palatine Hill. Instead he built two new palaces. The first was known as the Domus Transitoria (or Passageway) because it was designed as a link between the palace on the Palatine Hill and the imperial estate on the nearby Esquiline Hill. The Domus Transitoria was begun in A.D. 64 and probably lay unfinished when it was destroyed by the fire that occurred in the city later in the same year. This palace is known to have boasted a great courtyard into which a "wall of water" cascaded, flowing down steps and dividing into multiple murmuring falls before streaming through columnar openings into a pool. It is recorded that the finishes of this courtyard were luxurious, the walls and floor being inlaid with colored marble.

After the great fire in the city, Nero was able to take advantage of the disaster to acquire much of the damaged area as a site for a new imperial palace and park. The palace that he eventually built became known as the Domus Aurea (or Golden House), on account of the profusion of gold used in its decoration. In addition to a series

of garden courtyards, the palace enjoyed the setting of a park laid out in an informal landscape style on a scale unusually large for the tight confines of the city at that time.

The park was approached from the forum, or central square, of Rome along a ceremonial route known as the Via Sacra (or Sacred Way). This path was lined with colonnades and porticoes and ended in an entry area that was dominated by a colossal bronze statue of Nero, more than one hundred feet high. The park, thought to have covered an area of approximately 125 acres, was located in a valley between the Palatine and Esquiline Hills. As a result of the forty-mile-long aqueduct constructed during Claudius's reign, Nero was able to flood the valley to create a great lake as the focus of the new park. (Although the primary purpose of the aqueduct was to provide the city with a source of extra water, Nero was able to use his position to tap the supply for ornamental use.) The water was made to fall into the new lake via a row of monumental fountains. The finished park, an attempt to create a rural environment within the walls of the city, was described in the book *The Twelve Caesars* by the imperial biographer, Suetonius (A.D. ca. 69–ca. 140), as having "a pool which looked like the sea, surrounded by buildings which gave the impression of cities; besides there were rural areas with ploughed fields, vineyards, pastures, and woodlands, and filled with all types of domestic animals and beasts."

Inside the Golden House was one of Rome's characteristic imperial courtyard gardens. It featured a grotto that, like the park, illustrated the Roman skill in introducing a rural atmosphere into an urban setting. Of deliberately rustic appearance, the surface of the grotto was ornamented with a mixture of mosaic, glass, shell, and pumice-stone decorations. The emperor was unimpressed by his extravagant works upon their completion. According to Suetonius's biography of Nero, the emperor remarked simply that he had "at last begun to live like a human being." However, the Roman populace thought differently of his ostentation. He was forced to flee the city, after which his park was opened for public

Fig. 60.
Fresco from the House of Livia, at Prima Porta, now in the Terme Museum, Rome. Livia's villa was discovered and excavated in the nineteenth century, revealing a complete cycle of frescoes representing a garden. Behind a series of painted balustrades on the walls' lower levels was depicted an extraordinary range of garden flora and fauna.

use and eventually broken up. The Colosseum, the great Roman amphitheater, was subsequently built on part of the park's former site.

Domitian (r. A.D. 81–96) • One of Domitian's predecessors as emperor, Vespasian (r. A.D. 69–79), seems not to have lived on the Palatine. He preferred to inhabit the famous gardens made by Sallust near the Esquiline Hill during the Roman Republic, which had become part of the imperial estate by the time of Vespasian's reign. Domitian therefore erected a new palace and gardens for himself on the Palatine. The complex covered an area of approximately twelve and a half acres and was divided into two sections. The first section contained the public and ceremonial rooms and was known as the Domus Flavia, as Domitian hailed from the Flavian dynasty. The second section was the private residential area known as the Domus Augustana in honor of the first emperor.

The Domus Flavia, which stood on a level platform on the top of the hill, was entirely enclosed by a monumental yet elegant colonnade. Like previous palaces, it was designed around a great central courtyard with a fountain. Opening off the state banquet room was a second but smaller courtyard with a pair of fountains, oval in shape and of distinctive design. The floor of one of the pools seems to have been decorated with a maze-type pattern.

The private residence, which was approached separately through colonnaded courtyards, was at a lower, connected level. The residence boasted a series of internal courtyards that were ornamented by fountains and elaborate mosaic-lined pools. Accessed through these courtyards was the private residence's main garden. The most innovative of this garden's spaces was that designed in the shape of a hippodrome. Two semicircular pools decorated either end of the garden, their placement and design imitating the horses' turning points during a race in a functioning hippodrome. However, Domitian was murdered in A.D. 96 just as the Roman Empire was reaching the height of its power and prestige, and the development of this particular palace and its gardens was halted.

In addition to using the gardens on the Palatine Hill, later emperors enjoyed the use of the park on the neighboring Esquiline Hill. These gardens served as a quiet retreat from the official palace and were especially prized on account of the abundance of water available for their ornament, as most of the aqueducts entered Rome in the gardens' vicinity.

IMPERIAL VILLA GARDENS

The Early Emperors • Many emperors had rural retreats for occasional relaxation, or—as in the case of Tiberius—for retirement, away from the cares of empire. These rural villa gardens have survived far better than their urban counterparts, as they have been mostly undisturbed for centuries.

Augustus's wife, Livia, had such a rural villa at Prima Porta, just outside Rome. Its principal remains consist of a room whose frescoed walls display a continuous panoramic view of what appears to be a natural, flowering meadow. The painted plants are freely arranged, with little of the elaborate architectural or ornamental framework found in later garden frescoes. This may indicate that the gardens of the Augustan period, even the imperial ones, were characterized by an austere simplicity of planting and design (figs. 60, 61).

In contrast, Tiberius displayed his luxurious sensibility fully after his early withdrawal from Rome in A.D. 27. He chose to retire to (but still rule from) an imperial estate that had been acquired by Augustus on Capri, an island in the Bay of Naples (see fig. 17). Tiberius's projects were characterized by the unusual and dramatic locations in which he chose to carry them out. A villa perched on a cliff top and a banquet room in a sea cave were just two of these projects. The cliff-top villa posed exceptional problems for construction and water supply, the latter being stored in large underground cisterns that were covered with mosaic paving at the center of the villa. This was a highly personal villa complex in which little expense was spared in order to create a maritime residence with unmatched views over the sea and the surrounding countryside. The

natural cave adapted as a banquet room was at nearby Sperlonga (fig. 62; see also fig. 14). Through the artificial enlargement of the cave, ample space for luxurious dining was created. Much of the cave floor was artfully decorated with a series of ornamental pools. To complete the unique dining atmosphere, a set of statuary illustrating events from the Greek epic *The Odyssey* was commissioned (fig. 63). The daring of Tiberius's cave construction nearly ended in disaster when part of the roof fell in, just missing the emperor as he was dining.

Tiberius's taste for luxury extended to his vegetable garden. He had himself supplied with cucumbers out of season by having them planted in wheeled trolleys, which were pushed outside during the day and wheeled inside at night. The cucumbers thus grew earlier and lasted longer than in their normal season.

Tiberius's successor, Caligula (r. A.D. 37–41), preferred to take his relaxation not in a villa but afloat. Among his notorious architectural follies were the seagoing vessels he had built as luxurious floating palaces with gardens. Suetonius wrote of them in *The Twelve Caesars*: "He also constructed ten-oared galleys with sterns studded with gems, multicolored sails, and ample space for baths, verandas, and dining alcoves, and with a great variety of vines and fruit-bearing trees; reclining on these ships all day long he would sail along the Campanian coast amid choral dancing and singing." Caligula had floating palaces and gardens built on Lake Nemi in the Alban Hills outside of Rome. Domitian also favored retreating to the Alban Hills for relaxation. He enjoyed a large villa on the shores of the neighboring Lake Albano. It was filled with his impressive collection of Greek works of art. Only traces of this villa and its theater and *nymphaeum* remain.

Fig. 61.
Engraving of the House of Livia. This nineteenth-century engraving of the frescoes at Livia's villa at Prima Porta, by an anonymous artist, clearly depicts the freely arranged plants in the paintings.

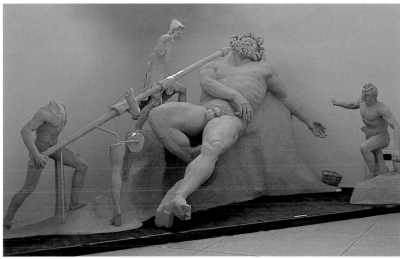

Fig. 62.
Sperlonga, near Naples. Tiberius's summer banquet room adapted from a natural cave was typical of his lavish construction projects.

Fig. 63.
Sculpture in the Sperlonga Museum. These figures, from a sculptural group depicting the stories of Homer's *Odyssey* originally located in Tiberius's cave, represent Ulysses and his companions blinding the giant Polyphemus.

Figs. 64–66.
The Canopus at Hadrian's Villa, Tivoli. The best-preserved of the palace's water gardens, the Canopus lies in the fold of a valley. Only part of its surrounding colonnade remains, but it appears to have had alternating flat and arched lintels. Framed by these remaining columns are stone figures of Mars, Mercury, and Minerva, which are reflected in the pool's still water. Flanking them are stone figures of Silenus, the drunken old satyr, who was often represented in gardens to convey a carefree atmosphere. Hadrian, a sophisticated man, was responsible for his garden's multicultural references.

Hadrian (r. A.D. 117–138) • Under Hadrian's predecessor, Trajan (r. A.D. 98–117), the Roman Empire reached its greatest geographical extent. Hadrian was the inheritor of vast public wealth. Much of it he spent on his villa at Tivoli outside Rome. When completed, it was the greatest Roman villa ever built and the largest in scope. Today it is the best-recorded and best-preserved of all the imperial villas.

Hadrian did not like Rome and spent much of his reign traveling throughout his empire, spending a considerable time in Greece. Greece was a country whose culture he adored and wished to see reflected in his villa. For an emperor, a palace in the city was a politically charged building, whose design he would be wise to make conform to some public norms. However,

in a country villa an emperor could create
a building and a garden with more freedom to
express his private personality. Hadrian exercised
this liberty fully at Tivoli to create a complex
of buildings and gardens with no predetermined
ground plan, no central focus, and no dominant
orientation. Its intricate layout loosely followed
the natural contours of the grounds, and
Hadrian's imagination and informed spontaneity
led to a great diversity and innovation in the
design of the area.

To study the complex's spaces is to study the
way in which its many distinct buildings and gardens formed part of an integrated whole. The
overall garden layout was not so much that of a
single garden but that of an elaborate group of
smaller individual gardens. Some of these were
directly linked to one another. Other areas were
isolated and could be reached only from the
villa's interior. Although each of the gardens had
a compositional integrity of its own, the gardens'
designs complemented each other to create a
sense of overall unity.

Most striking are those areas that were
designed by Hadrian to simulate the places that
most impressed him during his journeys in the
Eastern Empire. When his garden was complete,
Hadrian could choose to walk along his re-
creation of the Canopus canal, which he had seen
in Egypt. The banks of Hadrian's canal were lined
with copies of the caryatids—stone figures used
as columns—from the Erectheion temple on the
Athens Acropolis (figs. 64–67). Hadrian could
also stroll in the area of his park modeled on the
Vale of Tempe, the beautiful valley he admired
in Thessaly, in northern Greece. Yet another section of the villa featured a miniature copy of
the colonnade known as the Stoa Poikile, which
formed part of the ancient Athenian marketplace
(fig. 68). Thus in many parts of his garden,
Hadrian tried to capture the atmosphere of
his beloved Greece.

Figs. 67. ◁
The Canopus at Hadrian's Villa, Tivoli. Caryatids, inspired by the Erectheion on the Acropolis of Athens, stand along the side of the Canopus.

Fig. 68.
The Poecile at Hadrian's Villa. At Tivoli, Hadrian wished to symbolize or represent many different famous places in his empire. The Poecile is named after the famous Stoa Poikile of ancient Athens, where philosophers walked and debated. Only some of the walls of Hadrian's exercise galleries survive, but the large fishpond around which they were designed is intact.

However, the garden's features were not based exclusively on Greek or Near Eastern models. Some were Hadrian's unique architectural inventions. The design of some elements is so unusual that without written evidence it is impossible to determine their intended use. One such feature is the so-called Maritime Theater. Some scholars consider this structure to have been simply the emperor's personal retreat. Others believe it to have been an aviary and aquarium for the emperor's collection of rare birds and fish. Still others understand its complex shape to have had some cosmological significance. A circular island surrounded by a moat within a walled enclosure, it comprises an imaginative arrangement of elegant colonnades, courtyards, and fountains all doubled by reflection in the moat's waters. The effects of light and shade and of water, still and moving, must have been delightful (fig. 69).

Fig. 69.
The Maritime Theater at Hadrian's Villa, Tivoli. Enclosed within a 28-foot-high wall, this circular garden, created between A.D. 118 and 134, features a central islet pavilion, surrounded by a moat and a colonnade of forty Ionic columns. The islet was reached by two wooden bridges that were designed to turn on a central axis so that the islet could be isolated on occasion.

Most of the spaces within the villa and its grounds relied for their dramatic effect on the ornamental use of water, which was abundantly available from the nearby Sabine Hills. The center of the colonnaded courtyard known today as the Piazza d'Oro was occupied by a long canal extending at one end into an ornamental grotto with many fountain niches (figs. 70–73). The sight and sounds of water within this enclosed space must have been enchanting. Furthermore, an unusual semicircular garden with a large ornate fountain could be viewed from the state dining room. The roar and flash of its waters would have made a mighty impression on the diners.

The villa complex, begun in circa A.D. 118, eventually stretched over an area of about 150 acres. A novel feature was the pervasive use of curvilinear as well as rectilinear forms in its design. The use of curvilinear forms had been anticipated in the oval fountains in the courtyard of Domitian's palace on the Palatine Hill and subsequently reached its apogee in the lavishly free-form plan of the sophisticated villa excavated at Piazza Armerina in Sicily (see pp. 72–75).

Fig. 70.
The Piazza d'Oro at Hadrian's Villa, Tivoli. This title was given to this part of the villa during the Renaissance on account of the large number of rich objects excavated there. The area consisted of an extensive courtyard surrounded by covered colonnades. Opening off the colonnades was a series of elegant reception rooms of sophisticated and innovative architectural design and decoration.

Fig. 71.
Hadrian's Villa, Tivoli. Simple mosaics in black-and-white geometric patterns illustrate Hadrian's sometimes restrained taste. These designs are in strong contrast to the multicolored representational mosaics discovered in villas in Sicily and North Africa.

Fig. 72.
Mosaic floor design from the Piazza d'Oro at Hadrian's Villa, Tivoli. A complex geometry resulting in illusionistic patterns characterizes many of this site's mosaics.

Fig. 73.
The Library Courtyard at Hadrian's Villa, Tivoli. The villa is a site rich in innovative courtyard garden design. The water channel in this courtyard is terminated at either end by an unusual octagonal pool similar to those more familiar to us from Islamic garden design.

Fig. 74. ◁
Mosaic from the *frigidarium* of the baths at Piazza Armerina, Sicily. Garden pools were often lined with mosaics depicting appropriate marine themes, but few examples survive. The decoration of this bathhouse suggests what the mosaics of garden pools may have looked like.

Fig. 75. △
Mosaic from Piazza Armerina, Sicily. Beating game into a net is one of the oldest forms of hunting as a sport.

The Later Emperors • Hadrian's Villa and its gardens were probably not the result of a comprehensive plan. Rather, the final shape of the complex evolved slowly as the work progressed. This appears to have been the case also with the great villa at Piazza Armerina in Sicily. Although it is not known for whom this villa and its gardens were made, the site's scale and sophistication are equal to that of an imperial villa. The Piazza Armerina is more compact than Hadrian's Villa (the wealth of the empire was by then in decline), but its free and organic ground plan, architectural invention, and emphasis on curvilinear forms are as striking as those at Tivoli.

The chief garden features are the three colonnaded courtyards enclosed within the villa. The first is an entry courtyard, whose polygonal shape is highly irregular in the context of the rigorous orthogonal geometry that characterized other imperial and aristocratic palaces. The second

courtyard is in an orthodox rectangular shape, but its central pool is unexpectedly elaborate in form: It consists of three interconnecting basins, the outer two being semicircular; the central basin has two curved extensions that swell out around a central fountain. The third courtyard is in the shape of a truncated oval, an unusually fresh form that testifies to the creative design that survived to the end of the empire. The many diverse areas of the villa, both internal and external, were united by the installation of one of the most extraordinary groups of floor mosaics in all antiquity (figs. 74–79).

The history of the Roman imperial villa garden parallels the architectural development of the villa itself in the growing complexity of its planning and ornament. Of particular note is the increasing technical ingenuity in the management of water, both running and still, to provide a wide range of fountains and other water features.

Fig. 76.
Mosaic from Piazza Armerina, Sicily. In ancient Rome, there was an association between the gymnasium and the garden. Exercise grounds, particularly in private country villas, were often shaded by formal tree plantations and surrounded by parterres to create an elegant environment for gymnasts like those depicted in this mosaic.

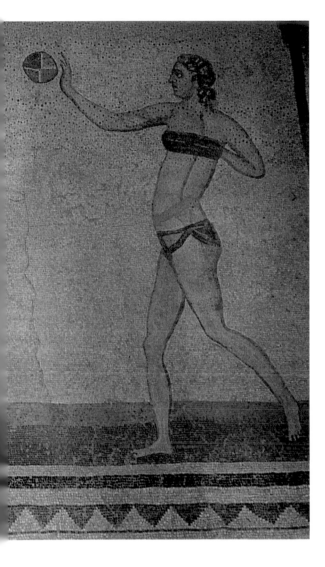

Fig. 77. ◁
Mosaic from Piazza Armerina, Sicily. Large ornamental fishponds stocked with a variety of fish were a feature of great villa parks. This mosaic depicts such a pond backed by an elegant columnar pavilion. Putti in elegant boats enjoy the sport of fishing

Figs. 78–79. ▷
Details of mosaics from Piazza Armerina, Sicily. The villa's exercise gallery is paved with mosaics depicting exotic animals like this ostrich and elephant, reminding us that the Roman interest in such creatures extended to the creation of ornamental menageries in the parks of luxurious villas.

CITY GARDENS

The cities of ancient Rome boasted numerous gardens, so many of which have been excavated and are known to us today that, taken as a group, they represent perhaps the greatest tradition of urban garden design in the world. Our knowledge of these gardens is particularly enhanced by the partial preservation of gardens in the cities of Herculaneum and Pompeii. However, these were gardens of provincial cities, and their owners were mostly merchants and professional men. These gardens therefore may not be a reliable guide to the high style of the capital city of Rome, in which great imperial and aristocratic gardens abounded but have not survived.

The construction of city gardens depended on the development of the cities themselves and of the domestic houses within them. Before the fifth century B.C., Roman cities were characterized by an informal, apparently haphazard, organization. Later cities, laid out under Greek influence, were planned according to a carefully organized rectangular grid system. Within the grid, house plots were austere and somewhat regimental in design.

Confined within walls, cities developed as inward-looking units. Their individual houses also faced inward, onto their own private open courts (figs. 80, 81). The open court, or atrium, was the principal source of light and air for the dwellings. By the second century B.C., the atrium was also being used for rainwater collection. Rainwater splashed down from an opening in the roof into a central depression known as an *impluvium*,

Fig. 80.
The House of the Labyrinth, Pompeii. This view from the entry courtyard into the garden would not have been available originally. It exists today because the walls of the reception room that stood between the two are ruined. Note the sunken rainwater trough in the entry courtyard and the covered colonnade that surrounded the garden. The red poppies are a weed that grows in cultivated ground and not part of an original planting.

which had been made in the courtyard floor (fig. 82). It was then led into a storage cistern located directly underneath, from which the water was drawn by the household for its daily needs during the dry season. Because the surface of the atrium was functional in this regard, it was necessary to keep it clear of impediments such as flower beds, pools, and garden sculpture. However, some atriums were decorated with mosaic paving. Plants, either decorative or culinary, were occasionally grown in judiciously placed pots, which themselves were sometimes ornamental rather than purely functional.

Fig. 81. △
The House of the Labyrinth, Pompeii. The pattern of a mosaic labyrinth discovered in one of the reception rooms of the house has been adapted in the modern box hedging to fill the vacant garden space.

Fig. 82. ▷
The House of the Silver Wedding, Pompeii. A double-height atrium imparts a noble scale to the town house of an ancient Pompeian family. Note the sunken trough into which rainwater from the roof spilled before being carried off underground into the house's storage tank. This house derives its name from the fact that its excavation began in 1893, the silver wedding anniversary of the then king of Italy, Umberto I (d. 1900).

After the construction of aqueducts and the provision of a public water supply in some cities, individual water storage in each household became less necessary. Atriums then began to develop more of a garden character. Small fountains and pools, as well as sculpture, were inserted (fig. 83). Nonetheless, such objects were usually raised on pedestals to safeguard the water storage system should it prove necessary in the future (figs. 84, 85).

Fig. 83. △
The House of Julia Felix, Pompeii. This pool has many recesses of both rectangular and semicircular shapes, in addition to square holes inset in its side walls. Lined in stone, the recesses were used by fish to breed. Although this appears to be one pool, it is actually divided into three distinct sections, which allowed for separating fish of differing maturity or species. Occasionally the owners became attached to their fish, which would come on call to be fed.

Fig. 84. ◁
The House of the Faun, Pompeii. The atrium is centered around a decorative trough for rainwater. Note the trough's carved marble sides and the multicolored cubical tile patterns that line its base. Found in 1830, the bronze figure known as the Dancing Faun, subsequently much copied, gave the house its name.

Fig. 85. ▷
The House of the Faun, Pompeii. The first courtyard garden was surrounded by colonnaded corridors and rooms. Native oleander, box (*Buxus sempervirens*), and daisy have been planted to approximate the courtyard's original planting.

A feeling of confinement often resulted from the inward-looking arrangement of the typical Roman house. This was sometimes mitigated by the use of illusionistic paintings on the walls of the house and of the garden, as mentioned in chapter one. These works created a sense of wider horizons and greater space by depicting extensions of the garden, or rural or exotic landscapes. These paintings offered a form of escapism for their owners from the often cramped reality of their everyday lives (figs. 86–89).

In addition to the atrium, many city houses boasted a second open or garden space. This was located to the rear of the house and was used during the early period of urban development as a basic kitchen garden with some rows of vegetables and fruit trees. This arrangement typified houses of the early Roman Republic at the end of the fourth and the beginning of the third centuries B.C. As public fruit and vegetable markets developed in the cities, however, it was no longer essential to have a private kitchen garden behind

Fig. 86.
The House of the Marine Venus, Pompeii. The scale and spatial arrangement of a typical Pompeian city garden is illustrated here. On the rear wall of the garden are frescoes of garden scenes and a depiction of Venus and her seashell, after which the house is now named.

Fig. 87.
Fresco from the House of the Marine Venus, Pompeii. Full-length figure of the god Mars, illustrating the Roman use of statuary in a garden setting.

Fig. 88.
Fresco from the House of the Marine Venus, Pompeii. A pedestal bowl or urn fountain of this kind frequently adorned the gardens of ancient Rome.

a city house. In many cases, wealthy urban families enjoyed the ownership of suburban or rural gardens and farms from which produce could be supplied. In time, therefore, the kitchen garden became largely ornamental. Such a garden was often surrounded by a colonnade acting as a sheltered walkway and leading to a summer dining pavilion at the end of the garden. The pavilion was usually the garden's visual focus. In the most sophisticated homes, the dining room acted as the focal point not only of the garden but of an entire planned vista through the axial sequence of indoor and outdoor spaces.

In some gardens, a shrine or a fountain was erected on the end wall instead of a summer dining pavilion. A shrine usually took the form of a recess or wall niche in which a figure representing a god was placed. A wall fountain sometimes took the form of a grotto, with rustic decorations mimicking a natural spring found in the countryside.

A key feature of an urban garden was the symmetry of both its general design and its details. The overall plan of a house, in the sequence of its rooms, courtyards, and gardens, was developed along axial lines. Because of the strict axiality and symmetry of its design, the House of the Faun, constructed about 180 B.C., is often regarded as the most finely planned house

and garden surviving at Pompeii (see figs. 84, 85). Symmetry often characterized the design of a garden itself, as in the layout of the narrow canals and pools, pergolas, and arbors of the garden of the House of Loreius Tiburtinus, also at Pompeii (see figs. 1, 95). Symmetry was a priority in the placing of objects such as marble and bronze statuary and other ornaments, as can be seen in the garden of the House of the Vettii in Pompeii (figs. 90–94).

Fig. 90.
The House of the Vettii, Pompeii. Flaming lamps light the way from the house into the garden and illustrate the close relationship between the design of the exterior and interior spaces of a Roman urban house.

Fig. 89. ◁
The House of Apollo, Pompeii. Although this house is famous for its fresco of Apollo, Venus, and Hesperus (goddess of the evening), it had a surprisingly modest garden. What remains of its garden colonnade looks today like a rustic cottage. Originally, it appeared to be much larger as a result of the illusionistic garden paintings that covered its high surrounding walls. According to one source, the garden boasted not only the well seen in this picture but also a fountain in the form of a freestanding stone centerpiece with four stepped slopes down which water cascaded.

Fig. 91. ◁
The House of the Vettii, Pompeii. This fresco shrine shows a pair of household gods flanking a lady as she makes a sacrifice to the guardian spirit of the house. The guardian spirit was frequently depicted, as here, in the form of a great coiling snake.

Fig. 92. ▷
The House of the Vettii, Pompeii. The garden was surrounded by a colonnade whose stone columns were covered with fluted white plaster to simulate marble. The interior wall of the colonnade was decorated with brilliantly colored frescoes (see fig. 90). On excavation, the garden's paths and beds were found to be surprisingly intact, making it possible to reconstruct their original curvilinear lines exactly. An abundance, almost a surfeit, of garden ornaments, both in marble and bronze, was also revealed. Raised marble basins, some plain, some elegantly shaped, and still others decorated with rich carvings and flutings, vie for attention with bronze and marble busts on low pillars.

Fig. 93. ▷
The House of the Vettii, Pompeii. Among other sculptures, bronze putti carry ducks as if to bring them to drink in one of the marble basins.

Fig. 94. ▷ ▷
Lithograph of the House of the Vettii, Pompeii. Fausto and Felice Niccolini produced a series of romantic drawings and prints of Pompeii between 1854 and 1896. This lithograph of the Vettii garden illustrates the fact that such gardens relied for their ornamental effect on sculpture, furniture, and fountains as well as on plants.

Fig. 95.
The House of Loreius Tiburtinus, Pompeii. The sloping garden behind the house features a tee-shaped canal on two levels. The upper arm of the canal leads the eye to a central pumice-lined niche (fig. 96) with a pedestal that formerly featured a figure of a kneeling youth carrying a jar, from which water flowed into the basin below. The basin is flanked by two dining couches, indicating that vessels may have been floated on the water's surface to keep the food and drink contained in them refreshingly cool. (See also fig. 1.)

Fig. 96.
The House of Loreius Tiburtinus, Pompeii. The upper canal in this garden is focused on this niche inlaid with pumice to look like a grotto. Two flanking frescoes depict mythological scenes.

The introduction of aqueducts and public water supplies to some cities from the Augustan period on allowed the Romans to incorporate many elaborate water features into their gardens, an option that was not available to the Greeks (figs. 95, 96). The readier supply of water also enabled the Romans to install new and more luxurious garden plantings.

Another key characteristic of the Roman urban garden was the liberal use of decorative sculpture. Such sculpture was particularly remarkable for its scale, always less than life-size, often small, even miniature. The garden of the House of the Vettii exemplifies its use (see figs. 93, 94). It is possible that this kind of lavish decoration reflects an acquisitiveness on the part of newly rich owners. It may otherwise reflect a desire to imitate, on a smaller urban scale, the extensive vistas lined with sculpture that were characteristic of country villa gardens. Indeed, the statuary in some urban gardens was deliberately chosen to evoke a rural atmosphere. Figures of gods and goddesses associated with the countryside, or figures of animal, birds, and fish, were frequently chosen (figs. 97–100).

Fig. 97.
Sculpture from the House of Loreius Tiburtinus, Pompeii. This marble fountain sculpture depicting Cupid seated on a rock and holding a theatrical mask was found at the center of the garden's lower canal.

Fig. 98. ◁
The House of the Stags, Herculaneum. This garden pavilion with pediment is approached through a symmetrically arranged group of furniture and garden sculpture of small scale. A pair of marble stags at bay, for which the house is now named, flanks a marble tripod table with circular top and lion-like legs. Another pair of figures depicts Hercules.

Fig. 99. △
Sculpture from the House of the Stags, Herculaneum. The young Hercules is shown with his lion skin and an upturned wine jar. As can be seen here, Hercules was sometimes depicted as inebriated.

Fig. 100. △
Sculpture from the House of the Stags, Herculaneum. The stag and hounds are depicted in a naturalistic style, the result of careful observation in nature.

A most intriguing aspect of urban gardens was the widespread use of hanging sculpture in the colonnades. Stone or bronze relief panels (*oscilli*) were displayed hanging on chains from the eaves (see figs. 37–39). Like most Roman sculpture, they were painted vividly with realistic color. Three-dimensional stone masks, often representative of characters from the theater, were sometimes hung in similar locations—an example of the close relationship between garden and theater design that has existed throughout the ages (see figs. 32, 34).

The planting of the Roman urban garden or courtyard is best evidenced from surviving wall frescoes of the period. The frescoes illustrate what we today refer to as "mixed borders," a judicious combination of small trees, shrubs, perennials, and bulbous plants arranged in informal tiers according to height and designed to be seen from the front. A typical planting was composed partly of evergreen plants for year-round effect and partly of deciduous plants for seasonal color. At the back of the border were taller trees, again in a mixture of evergreen and deciduous species. Among the evergreen cypresses and palm trees, a variety of fruit trees provided seasonal flower and fruit (figs. 101–3).

Although excellent evidence of the early Roman urban garden is provided by the excavations in the cities destroyed by the eruption of Vesuvius in A.D. 79, for later urban gardens one must go to some of the cities of the far Roman provinces or to the port city of Ostia, west of Rome. As with Pompeii, much of the urban

Fig. 101.
Fresco from the House of the Orchard, Pompeii. This modest house derives its name from the frescoes of fruit trees on its bedroom walls. Unusually, these works comprise individual tree and shrub portraits rather than the mixed plantings normally illustrated. Here both doves and pigeons perch on the branches of a fruit tree.

Fig. 102.
Fresco from the House of the Orchard, Pompeii. This fruit tree is depicted against a light blue background suggesting the sky.

Fig. 103.
Fresco from the House of the Orchard, Pompeii. This fresco includes a depiction of a *pinax* with its frame painted a brilliant red.

structure of Ostia is intact. It was not preserved by a catastrophic incident but rather was gradually abandoned for economic reasons. In the structure known as the House of Amor and Psyche, nearly half of the ground area is given over to the garden. Its focal point is a set of five fountain niches, lined with marble and glass mosaic and set against the property's rear wall. It is thought that water cascaded from figures in the niches and then splashed down short water ramps into semicircular pools. From these pools the water flowed through outlets, perhaps in the form of lions' masks, to be eventually led out of the garden. This elaborate architectural fountain, with its clear, confident monumentality, demonstrates how sophisticated small urban gardens of the late imperial period had become.

Other forms of city gardens also flourished. The town of Ostia was characterized not so much by individual houses as by apartment blocks. Most of these had communal gardens, which are recorded as having small statuary groups and fountains. Martial mentions the use of his window ledges as a location for growing plants, a practice that may have been popular with many apartment dwellers. Seneca makes reference to the existence of roof gardens in his time.

Fig. 104.
The Villa of Poppaea, Oplontis. This luxurious suburban villa near Pompeii, dating from circa A.D. 50, belonged to the family of Poppaea, wife of the emperor Nero. Country houses were often surrounded by columns and porticoes of different sizes overlooking gardens and the rural landscape surrounding them. The replanting of this garden was undertaken only after excavations revealed the precise location and types of plants originally used. The long horizontal line of the clipped box hedges is contrasted with the rhythmical planting of standard oleanders seen here in flower. Both the oleander and the box are Mediterranean natives.

VILLA GARDENS

Early Republican Roman country gardens consisted of simple crops of flowers, vegetables, and fruits grown in plots that usually required a water source or storage facility. A villa at Settefinestre, north of Rome, from 75 B.C., featured an early ornamental garden with an atrium, a peristyle, and a portico from which to look out over the countryside. On one side of the villa were three large walled gardens, probably kitchen gardens, and beyond was a larger, detached walled area, probably an orchard. As Rome became a great power, the increase in wealth brought about changes in Roman upper-class customs, one of which was the desire to acquire a rural villa.

Villa gardens can be divided into three types based on location: the suburban villa, the country villa, and the maritime villa. From the second century B.C. on, wealthy citizens owned suburban villas just outside a city's walls (figs. 104–10). Many of the roads leading out of Pompeii were lined with extensive suburban residences. The fact that people were prepared to expend large amounts of time and money on building villas outside the protective walls of towns was an indication of the benign social and political situation of the time. The suburban Villa of the Mysteries, located 120 yards outside the walls of Pompeii and dating from the mid-first century A.D., occupied an area of approximately one and a half acres. The arrangement of rooms and gardens was the reverse of that in nearby city dwellings. Whereas in a city house the front door usually opened to an atrium and then to a peristyle at the back, this villa's front door opened directly onto the peristyle, which led in turn to the atrium.

By the end of the Roman Republic (27 B.C.), many wealthy Romans had acquired large agricultural estates from which they derived regular income. The supervision of these estates required a regular exodus by the owners and their families from the city during the sowing and reaping seasons, in particular. Villas, often luxurious, were built on the farms for their accommodation. In addition, gardens were often laid out for the visitors' delight during their short stay.

Fig. 105.
Fresco from the Villa of
Poppaea, Oplontis. A fantasy
garden is illustrated on the
walls of the villa's dining
room, featuring a typical
Roman fountain in the form
of a twin-handled stone basin
on a raised pedestal. While in
many such basins a small jet
of water would play, others,
like the one shown here, functioned as simple birdbaths.
Note the decorative fluting on
the bowl and the spiral fluting
carved on the pedestal. The
background vegetation resem-
bles myrtle, a Mediterranean
native, which we know from
literary sources was often
planted in Roman gardens.

Fig. 106.
Fresco from the Villa of Poppaea, Oplontis. Depiction of a fountain with a fluted bowl in an unusual rectangular shape. Its pedestal in the form of a kneeling winged figure is also exceptional.

Fig. 107.
Fresco from the Villa of Poppaea, Oplontis. A painting of a pair of projecting columns, one painted in false marble, the other enriched with gilded tendrils, illustrates the sumptuous nature of the villa's decoration. Between the columns is an elegant incense burner of gilded bronze.

Fig. 108.
The Villa of Diomedes, Pompeii. The vestigial columns of a domestic temple are seen at the heart of a typically verdant villa garden.

Fig. 109.
The Villa of Diomedes, Pompeii. This pedestal in the form of a fluted and truncated marble column is located by the garden's small domestic temple.

The country villa was similar to the city house in that it had internal courts and gardens. However, the rural home usually had external porticoes and colonnades, terraces, and gardens facing outward over a view. Although a villa, like a city house, was planned in an axial, symmetrical sequence of rooms, courts, and gardens, there was greater freedom in the design of these elements because of the increased space available. Beyond the garden around the villa, the view often included a working agricultural estate laid out in a carefully planned grid of fields and, beyond that, distant mountains or hills. Life for the owner and his family on a Roman rural estate was very much as it has been ever since—pleasant hours spent hunting, relaxing, eating, studying, and drinking in the open air while the day-to-day agricultural and economic activities of the estate took place around them (figs. 111–116).

Fig. 110.
The Villa of Diomedes, Pompeii. Located immediately outside Pompeii's city walls, the villa's large garden had views over the countryside to the sea. The stately rhythm of the pillars, seventeen on each of the garden's four sides, underlines the bold scale of this suburban garden.

Fig. 111.
The Grotto of Catullus, Lake Garda. This villa derives its name from the belief that it may have belonged to the family of the well-known poet Catullus (ca. 84 – ca. 54 B.C.). The villa's site enjoys a mild winter climate, refreshing summer breezes, and spectacular views over the lake. Warm sulfur springs rise from the shallows of the lake below the villa. These would have added greatly to the attraction of the site for the Romans, for whom bathing was a constant activity.

Fig. 112.
The Grotto of Catullus, Lake Garda. The olive grove planted around the villa re-creates the atmosphere of wooded seclusion that the villa, isolated at the end of its promontory, originally enjoyed.

Pliny the Younger mentions the desirability of the creation of long promenades and driveways for outings in the countryside. However, the Roman appreciation was not for the natural landscape but for the landscape as "improved" by the hand of man. Indeed, the artificial enhancement of nature was a constant activity. Natural springs, caves, grottoes, and groves were often enhanced by ornamental, sometimes sacred, structures in the form of shrines, pavilions, urns, and fountains.

The planting on a country estate would appear, if the evidence of frescoes is taken into account, to be mainly of native pine and cypress. The cypress, in particular, was very adaptable in its uses. It was often closely planted to give wind shelter as well as to give deep shade where this was desired. Sometimes it was clipped into dense, high hedges. In other instances, it was, as Pliny the Elder wrote in his *Natural History*, "evenly rounded off with trim slenderness" to make those tall columnar forms that have characterized the Tuscan landscape since. However, the most widely used tree for ornamental planting within the confines of a country estate was the oriental plane tree, a native not of Italy but of the Near East. We know it was widely planted in avenues as well as in simple lines and in groves.

Fig. 113.
The Grotto of Catullus, Lake Garda. One of the grandest private villas of ancient Rome, it boasted an ambulatory, or covered gallery, for indoor exercise next to one of the villa's internal courtyard gardens. Only some of the central columns of the ambulatory remain.

The development of aqueducts—in this case private aqueducts—led to the increased use of pools, fountains, and fishponds in country gardens. On some estates, fishponds became so large and so numerous that they were in reality large, commercial fish farms rather than ornamental features. Nonetheless, the jets that kept the water in these ponds aerated were quite decorative.

A detailed account of such an elaborate rural villa garden survives in Pliny the Younger's *Letters*, which describes his property in Tuscany set in the middle of an agricultural estate, the principal cash crop of which was grapes. His terraced and colonnaded villa faced south and appears to have doubled as a hunting lodge. It was located, he wrote, "at the foot of the Apennines . . . where the great spreading plain is ringed with mountains, their tops crowned by ancient woods of tall trees,

Fig. 114. △
The Grotto of Catullus, Lake Garda. Unlike some imperial villas with their irregular overall plans, this villa and its gardens were designed with a single symmetrical plan, which focused on a principal reception room with a colonnaded loggia and a garden terrace overlooking the water.

Fig. 115. ◁
Horace's Farm, Licenza. The poet Horace was critical of luxurious villas and gardens. His preference was for simpler rural dwellings surrounded by modest groves of trees, orchards, and vegetable gardens. Although this villa known as Horace's Farm may not have been the exact villa in the Sabine Hills used by Horace, it serves as a model for his ideal rural retreat.

Fig. 116. ▷
Horace's Farm, Licenza. The villa's mosaic-floored rooms are arranged around an open courtyard with a square pool (now with a wooden fence) and are raised above an adjoining oblong garden containing a swimming pool in the center. A spring within earshot of the villa is thought perhaps to be the "Bandusian spring" referred to by Horace in his poetry. In the background is the present-day hill town of Licenza.

Fig. 117.
View from a villa at Tyndaris, Sicily. Curiosities of nature appealed to the inquiring Roman mind. This town overlooked attractive shifting formations of sand and gravel produced by unusual currents in the shallows at the foot of the cliff.

where there is a good deal of mixed hunting to be had." Each room in the villa and each space in the garden is described in terms of its orientation to the prevailing winds, its suitability for winter or summer use, and its location within the villa complex from the point of view of noise or seclusion.

Pliny went on to describe the villa's terrace of geometrical box topiary and the bank below, on which there were figures of animals cut in box. The figures faced each other on either side of a vista. Below them was a bed of acanthus "so soft one could say it looks like water" (the

acanthus was used by the Romans as a lush ground covering in shady areas of the garden). Pliny specifically mentions a room, perhaps a garden pavilion, that was constructed in the shadow of a great plane tree. Inside the pavilion was a small fountain bowl ringed with tiny jets making a lovely murmuring sound. The room's decoration was completed by a fresco depicting birds perched on the branches of trees.

Pliny especially enjoyed the view over the countryside from the villa and its garden, comparing it to a beautiful landscape painting. This effect was augmented by the garden's design, which became increasingly naturalistic as it receded from the villa to join the natural landscape around its edges. Although we tend to think of the Romans as urban beings primarily, Pliny's account evidences the affection that they also felt for the countryside.

Maritime or coastal villas were not centers of agricultural production since the coastal soils, being rocky or sandy, were not very fertile. These villas were laid out mainly for pleasure, evidence of the increasing luxury enjoyed by Romans during the imperial period (figs. 117–19). Wealthy Romans vied for airy sites with panoramic views along the coasts of Latium and Campania for their luxury seaside villas. The coastal villa served mainly as a residence in winter and spring, when the mild, maritime climate could be enjoyed from the open terraces and garden promenades around it. Both villa and garden were laid out with an orientation protecting them from the gales that would on occasion send sea spray beating against the villa's walls. Despite the need for protection from wind, a maritime villa was open in plan, its rooms interlocking with outdoor courts and gardens, and the planting was designed to thrive in a maritime environment.

After Augustus acquired a maritime estate on the island of Capri, the Bay of Naples became ringed with the luxurious villas of the Roman aristocracy. Cicero had a villa on the seashore at Gaeta. Maritime villas, having no practical function and being designed as leisure complexes only, provided ideal opportunities for imaginative architectural experiment. The villas often took the form of a single-story colonnaded pavilion running between two-story corner towers. Extending in front of the colonnades were raised terraces, along which the villa's occupants might enjoy the winter sun as well as cool breezes in summer. Sometimes the colonnades were decorated with a central portico and were reflected in a sheet of water, the pool forming the axis of a large formal garden.

A description of a garden in such a villa has been left to us by Pliny the Younger in his account of his own villa of Laurentum on the coast near Ostia (see pp. 2–3). It was located on the seashore within reach of the sea spray and

enjoyed views of the water from many sides. He wrote of the pleasures of its breezy terrace during hot weather and described its garden as having walks lined with box, rosemary, vines, blackberries, and figs.

Pliny owned another two villas on Lake Como in the north of Italy. He wrote in his *Letters* of their having contrasting locations: "The former has a wide view of the lake, the latter a closer one as it is built to curve around a single bay, following its line with a broad terrace, while the other stands on a high ridge separating two bays." Unfortunately, he wrote little more about them. However, considerable excavation has taken place on a site overlooking the lake, which is thought to be the location of one of these villas.

Roman villas and their gardens continued to be built, sometimes at considerable expense, well into the fourth and fifth centuries A.D., even though by that time the empire was in terminal decline.

Fig. 118.
Mosaic from a villa at Tyndaris, Sicily. One of the Tyndaris houses has a mosaic floor incorporating the "triskelion" symbol consisting of three legs radiating from a common center. The use of this symbol, which originated in ancient Greece, together with the Hellenistic sculptures found on-site, testify to the Greek influence on this town.

Fig. 119.
A villa at Tyndaris, Sicily. This isolated hill town overlooked a once-important river port. Pliny recorded how much of the town had fallen down the cliff into the sea during an earthquake. Excavations have partially uncovered some of the town's houses and gardens.

SACRED GARDENS AND GROVES

During the early Roman Republic, a small number of trees—remnants of Rome's original forest—survived within the city's walls. Some of these trees were associated with ancient religious rites and so were protected from being cut. Toward the end of the Republic there was a decline in ancient beliefs, and many of these trees were felled; still, certain groves of trees did survive. These were sacred groves in which shrines and grottoes, as well as tombs and other memorials, had been erected among the trees. Later, other sites within the city were planted with trees and treated as memorial or sacred groves. Augustus planted a memorial grove after the death of two of his grandchildren, and his own mausoleum was surrounded by a park with trees.

Such memorial groves were not solely the prerogative of the imperial family. Cicero wrote of his search for a suitable place to plant a grove in honor of his dead daughter. Indeed, many wealthy families maintained sacred groves in a city's suburbs or in the countryside. These sites were furnished with shrines to the family's favorite gods as well as with family memorials. The penalty for cutting down a tree in such a grove was often death. However, trees were not sacred only when they formed part of memorial groves. A single tree might be dedicated by its owner to a god. Horace had a great pine tree dedicated to the goddess Diana in his garden in the Sabine Hills.

Pious people in rural communities often devised "spontaneous" gardens around altars and memorial stones or columns that they found in the Roman countryside. Ownerless and sometimes even in ruin, such sites would become the focus of a local or personal cult. They were sometimes planted around with trees or shrubs as a mark of veneration and were refurnished constantly with fresh garlands of foliage and flowers. Such ad hoc sacred shrines are frequently depicted in what have become known as the "sacro-idyllic" landscape paintings of ancient Rome. Idealized paintings of this type were widespread on the walls of both villas and urban houses, even imperial residences, as evidenced by the examples from the House of Livia and the Room of the Masks in the House of Augustus, both on the Palatine Hill.

PUBLIC PARKS

The Roman tradition of planting trees in public urban areas may have derived from ancient Greece. We know that trees were planted in the Agora, or marketplace, of the city of Athens as early as the fifth century B.C. As the ancient Roman cities expanded, an awareness grew of the need for public parks within them. Vitruvius, writing in Augustus's time, recommended that trees be planted in city squares and temple precincts.

Agrippa, a consul at the time of Augustus, willed his gardens to the people of Rome. These gardens included a grove of plane trees furnished with statuary representing animals such as bears and lions. (Martial confirms the use of statues of wild beasts in public parks. He recounts one such statue of a bear represented as if growling in anger and relates a tragic incident in which his friend Hylas had jokingly put his hand in the bear's mouth one day, only to be fatally bitten by a snake that had been coiled up inside.) Agrippa's park also boasted two large sheets of water, one in the form of a great still pool, or *stagnum*, and the other a *euripus*, a canal of running water, perhaps fed by a spring or stream. These pools were the first in a Roman public park to have been supplied with water from an aqueduct. Between the two sheets of water, a fine statue of a lion acted as the garden's main focal point.

Unlike Agrippa's park, most of Rome's public parks were deliberately created as public gardens and were usually attached to public buildings such as theaters, baths, or temples. Rome's first substantial public park, called Pompey's Portico, was laid out circa 55 B.C. in front of Pompey's Theater by Pompey the Great, one of the last eminent consuls of the Roman Republic before the empire was established. This park introduced the design of most Roman public parks to follow, although inevitably there were variations depending on site, climate, and subsequent changes of taste. Pompey's Portico derived its name from the fact that the park was entirely surrounded by a series of continuous porticoes. In terms of the adjoining theater's function, they provided shade from the sun and shelter from the rain during the intervals between performances. The open area in the middle of the park was planted in formal rows of plane trees, with statues raised on plinths at intervals under the trees. Two rectangular sheets of water appear to have been positioned near the center of the space. Built-in seating recesses, alternately rectangular and semicircular in shape, completed the accommodations.

In the public park known as Livia's Portico in Rome, the walks were flanked by trelliswork arcades to provide side shade. Sometimes the open area at the center of a public garden as well as the shady porticoes were used as exercise yards known as palaestrae, the development of physique being an important part of Roman daily life. An almost complete example of a palaestra survives by the theater at Pompeii. The provision of public parks as adjuncts of theater complexes was also prevalent throughout the Roman provinces. Such remains are visible in the Roman sites of Mérida and Italica, both in present-day Spain.

Other public parks both in Rome itself and in the provinces were attached to bathing complexes. Nero is credited with the inauguration of this new public garden tradition. Large open areas attached to the Baths of Titus and the Baths of Trajan were laid out as arenas for pre- and postbathing leisure and exercise. In the gardens of some bathing complexes, large pools were surrounded by stone benches on which the public might sit. Although these gardens were usually located in internal courtyards, some—such as those of the Baths of Caracalla and the Baths of Diocletian (built A.D. 298–306)—also boasted peripheral garden areas between the building complex and the outer boundary wall.

The Roman concept of bathing in a garden was lavishly realized in the Baths of Stabies—even their internal bathing halls were painted with a garden theme. Provincial examples of public baths with gardens can be identified at such places as Conimbriga, Aphrodisias, and Thuburbo Majus in present-day Portugal, Turkey, and Tunisia, respectively.

Some public gardens were attached to temples, which were often surrounded by continuous covered colonnades, much as other public parks were. The open area in the middle of the temple precinct was usually planted with formal rows of plane trees around the temple itself. Examples in Rome included the park of Divius Claudius, the temple dedicated to the deified emperor Claudius; the park around the Temple of Peace; and the park of the Adonea, the precinct dedicated to the cult of Adonis, who was famed as the love of the goddess Venus. Sometimes trees believed to be appropriate for the temple deity were planted. As Pliny the Elder wrote, different tree species were perpetually dedicated to particular gods. It is thought that bay trees grew in the precincts of the great temple of Apollo at Didyma, near Miletus in present-day Turkey. A pair of myrtle trees grew in the precincts of the Temple of Romulus in Rome. In the absence of much evidence of planting within temple precincts from formal excavations, these isolated records merely hint about what such planting might have looked like.

Temple precincts were furnished with ceremonial columns, altars—sometimes elaborately designed and sculpted—at which sacrifices took place, and sundials, sometimes monumental in scale. These types of temple structures can be seen at the Temple of Apollo in Pompeii (figs. 42, 120). Occasionally, large statuary groups were included. Such a group was featured in the Forum Pacis, the public space in front of the Temple of Peace, or Ara Pacis, in Rome. It represented the Nile River, with the principal figure surrounded by figures of sixteen children, each representing one of the great river's tributaries. The same space, according to the historian Procopius (A.D. ca. 500–ca. 532), boasted a fountain in the form of a bronze bull.

MARKET GARDENS

We know that cities had been surrounded by market gardens since Greek times, for Aristotle mentioned a law providing for all household refuse to be carried out of Athens by civic collectors and used as manure on the market gardens outside the city walls. Commercial market gardens likewise surrounded Roman towns and cities. Most of them supplied a variety of produce, but others are recorded as specializing in the production of, for example, cucumbers, gourds, and melons, and still others specialized in growing flowers. Roses, narcissi, and violets are especially mentioned in the sources. These flowers were used in making the wreaths, garlands, and other floral decorations popular in ancient Rome.

One other kind of garden could also be seen in the suburbs of, and in the countryside around, the big cities. These were gardens attached to taverns. Extensively planted with shade trees, they were venues to which the citizens could escape during summer heat and especially during public holidays and summer festivals.

Fig. 120
The Temple of Apollo, Pompeii. Although much is known about private open spaces and gardens in Pompeii, much less is known about the design of public open spaces. This religious sanctuary from the second century B.C. was surrounded by a two-level covered colonnade, some of the lower portion of which remains. The focal point of the paved enclosure is a stone altar used for offerings. Behind it and to the right in this photograph is a concave sundial atop a tall white marble column, which was inserted during the later Augustan period (seen in fig. 42).

III

PROVINCIAL GARDENS:
FROM THE EASTERN EMPIRE TO BRITAIN

ROME BEGAN as a small city-state. However, by the end of the third century B.C., it had achieved domination over much of Italy and had laid the foundations of an empire abroad. During the second century B.C., the Greek world submitted to Rome's influence, and by the end of the century the whole of the Eastern Mediterranean world had fallen under her power. From 146 B.C. on, parts of Africa came under Roman control. Meanwhile, Rome was expanding to the west during the same period—Spain became hers in the second century B.C. Julius Caesar subdued Gaul (approximately present-day France) circa 50 B.C., and the Roman armies subsequently invaded Britain. Step by step, Rome's great empire was established and strengthened.

After each successive conquest, the Romans moved rapidly to consolidate their new power by instituting a civilian as well as a military infrastructure. Settlers, often retired Roman soldiers, were given land grants in the new province. The settlers were followed by an immigrant merchant population. Under the combined influence of these groups, the indigenous populations of the conquered territories were slowly but inevitably romanized. New public and domestic buildings in provincial cities began to follow Roman models and, later, to boast Roman-style gardens (figs. 121–23). These gardens were not simple replicas of Roman gardens in Italy. It was necessary to adapt their design and planting to local climates and to differing conditions within the far-flung empire.

As communications were considerably slower during this period than they are now, it took time for developments in horticultural techniques and garden design to travel from the imperial capital to the provinces. Many of the more interesting gardens in the Roman provinces date, therefore, to a later period in Roman history. Furthermore, because most of our knowledge about Roman gardens in Italy is based on the earlier period, late provincial gardens provide crucial historical information.

Sabratha, Libya. Figure of Venus shown set in a niche with a rectangular pool in front. See also fig. 130.

Fig. 121.
The Villa of the Voliere, Carthage. The simple courtyard with columns, modest in scale yet elegant in proportion, contrasts with the richly patterned floor of one of the villa's erstwhile rooms in the foreground.

Fig. 122.
The Villa of the Voliere, Carthage. Stone figures on plinths have been set up in the garden's surrounding colonnade.

Fig. 123.
The Villa of the Voliere, Carthage. Roman sculpture, including garden sculpture, was usually positioned in a location appropriate to its subject. Here a stone eagle is placed to be seen against the sky.

THE EASTERN EMPIRE

The area of Rome's Eastern Empire comprised present-day Greece, Turkey (then known generally as Asia Minor), Syria, and part of Arabia. The sack of Athens by the army of the Roman general Sulla (138–78 B.C.) in 86 B.C. terminated that city's period of greatness. The independence of the Greek city-states came to an end with the incorporation of the last Greek province into the Roman Empire nearly sixty years later, in 27 B.C.

Being admirers of Greek culture, the Romans made little attempt to impose their way of life onto their Greek subjects, and Greek architecture and design continued to be influential. As mentioned in chapter one, the Greeks had developed the colonnaded court concept for town house design, as seen in an early example that has been excavated at Kameiros, on the island of Rhodes. The Romans adopted this concept and eventually made it their own. The peristyle courtyard, or garden, as the colonnaded courtyard became known, seems to have been synonymous with mainstream Roman garden design.

A series of houses from the Hellenistic and Roman periods has been excavated on the island of Delos, which, although the smallest of the islands of the Cyclades, was once the political and religious center of the Aegean region. A composite picture of the typical Delian house and garden court can be built up by examining a number of these houses. Many have colonnaded courtyards, some with columns fabricated from luxurious marble, as the homes belonged to wealthy merchants. The atriums in these houses had colorful mosaic floors with water storage cisterns below. A decorative mosaic representing Dionysus, god of wine, wreathed in ivy leaves, is located in the floor of the courtyard of the House of Dionysus. A mosaic depicting a dolphin covers a cistern in the House of Cleopatra. This house's marble colonnade has been restored, and in the courtyard stand statues representing Cleopatra and Dioscourides, the house's Athenian owners in the second century B.C. In the same quarter of the city is the House of the Trident, one of the largest on the island. It has an atrium with an elegant wellhead through which water was drawn up from the cistern below. This house also boasted a type of colonnaded courtyard called a "Rhodian peristyle," whose design originated on the island of Rhodes. The Rhodian peristyle was characterized by an unusually high colonnade on one side of its courtyard, which served as the front of a single high-ceilinged room.

In the ancient city of Ephesus (located in present-day Turkey), several private houses have been excavated that were occupied from the first to the seventh century A.D. (fig. 124). The remains of a fountain survive in the center of one colonnaded courtyard that is graced by twenty-four blue marble Ionic columns. Another house has not one but two atriums, the larger of which boasts particularly fine Corinthian columns. The great treasure of this courtyard is its delicately beautiful glass mosaic dating from the fifth century A.D. Located in a niche, the mosaic depicts the heads of Dionysus and his bride, Ariadne, against a background of luxuriant foliage and surrounded by a glittering array of animals and birds. The mosaic conjures up a vision of an extraordinary natural paradise. As the light changes, the glass pieces sparkle and the figures in the mosaic appear to move, as though momentarily endowed with life.

Fig. 124.
Ephesus, Turkey. Although this city, one of the most important in the Roman province of Asia Minor, is best known for its elaborate civic buildings and monumental public fountains, the private houses that have been excavated bear some resemblance to those of Pompeii and Herculaneum from the first century A.D., with small paved courtyards, one of which has the remains of a fountain basin at its center. Today, the site still contains much volunteer vegetation, providing a better sense than many great Roman sites of the balance between stone and vegetation that must have been an original characteristic of Roman cities.

Fig. 125.
Villa Brioni, Croatia. The offshore Brioni Islands were a favorite location for the country villas of the citizens of Pula, a commercially important town on the Adriatic coast from the beginning of the first century A.D. This partially extant villa was raised on a platform, grassed today, so that its occupants could better enjoy sweeping coastal views.

Further south, the city of Dura-Europos sat on a plateau above the west bank of the Euphrates River, in present-day Syria. It was built under Severan emperors (Severus and his descendants; see p. 120) in the third century A.D. A palace, the largest building in the city, was built for the *dux ripae* (riverbank commander), who oversaw the Roman troops on this frontier of the empire. One entered the palace through two imposing colonnaded courtyards.

One of the most splendid garden developments was that commissioned by Herod the Great, King of Judaea, before his death in 4 B.C. (Judaea became a province of Rome in A.D. 6.) Herod, an admirer of Roman culture, constructed a great palace known as Masada on a rock overlooking the Dead Sea (a site located in present-day Israel). What is known today as the Northern Palace is graced with three descending garden terraces, the uppermost surrounded by a semi-circular colonnade. The middle terrace had a

circular pavilion backed by a covered portico, while on the lowest terrace a belvedere provided a gorgeous view of the valley below.

Finally, the provinces of Pannonia (present-day Hungary) and Illyria (present-day Croatia), on the northern fringes of eastern Europe, should not be neglected. Outside the modern city of Budapest, town houses with ornamental court-yards have been excavated in the Roman town known as Aquincum, once an important commu-nity on the frontier of the empire. Along the

Dalmatian coast of Croatia on the island of Brioni Grande, an extensive maritime villa with interlinked gardens and courts has been excavated (figs. 125–27). Further south on the coast is Split and its great palace to which the emperor Diocletian (r. A.D. 284–305) retired. Although no archaeological evidence of a garden exists there, Diocletian was an enthusiastic gardener. He is known to have grown excellent cabbages with his own hand.

Fig. 126.
Villa Brioni, Croatia. A circular courtyard pool is sur-rounded by a raised stone ledge set with sinuous curves in the courtyard corners.

Fig. 127.
Villa Brioni, Croatia. Deer grazing
in the background of the villa and
its colonnade evoke for today's
visitor the hunting parks that
formed an integral part of many
Roman country estates.

AFRICA

The Roman province in Africa comprised a vast territory stretching across the North African coast for a distance of about 1,250 miles and included the present-day countries of Morocco, Algeria, Tunisia, and Libya (figs. 128–33). Its annexation began after the Roman destruction of Carthage in 146 B.C. Africa's importance to Rome was as a source of food, producing great quantities of wheat, corn, barley, olives, and wine, a bounty that is difficult to imagine today as the fertility of the region has declined due to progressive desertification. The peak period of the province can be dated to the imperial reign of one of its sons, Septimius Severus (r. A.D. 193–211). Septimius was a considerable patron of his native city and province. He was born in Leptis Magna (in present-day Libya), one of the wealthiest cities in the Roman world at the end of the second century A.D. (figs. 134–40). After the murder of the last emperor of the Severan dynasty, Alexander Severus, in A.D. 235, Africa's power as a province went into decline. However, its economy remained active until the late stages of Rome's empire, even when the Italian mainland had already sunk into anarchy.

Fig. 128. ▽
Sabratha, Libya. A pattern of alternating rectilinear and semicircular recesses decorates the face of the theater at this site. This pattern is characteristic of much Roman building and garden design. See, for example, the hedging pattern in the reconstructed Roman garden at Fishbourne in England (fig. 161).

Fig. 129. ▷
Sabratha, Libya. The Roman use of appropriately themed sculpture is illustrated by the white marble dolphin marking the end of the theater's *cavea* (auditorium) at this seaside site.

Fig. 130. ◁
Sabratha, Libya. Venus was associated with gardens but also with the sea. Here a figure of the goddess is set in an alcove overlooking the Mediterranean.

Fig. 131. ▷
Sabratha, Libya. The mosaic floor beyond the Venus niche illustrates the villa's location with panoramic views over the shoreline.

Fig. 132. △
Sabratha, Libya. The complex geometry of this niche's mosaic floor illustrates the artistic and technical sophistication of Roman sites in North Africa.

Fig. 133. ▷
Sabratha, Libya. One of a series of bas-reliefs in a provincial sculptural style, this work represents the Judgment of Paris with Venus as the victor, holding a golden apple.

Fig. 134. ▷
Leptis Magna, Libya. This stone table found in the market was supported, as were many garden tables, on the backs of stone-carved lions.

Fig. 135. △
Leptis Magna, Libya. The stone table of a market stall echoes a typical garden table, which was often supported by carved beasts, usually griffins. In this case, both a griffin and a dolphin have been used.

Fig. 136. ◁
Leptis Magna, Libya. Example of a typical stone bench in the bath buildings known as the Hadrianic Baths, smaller versions of which were used in the gardens.

Fig. 137. ▷
Leptis Magna, Libya. This stone balustrade in the basilica features the diamond lattice pattern popularly used for decorative walling in Roman gardens.

Fig. 139. ▷
Leptis Magna, Libya. Stone masks, like that shown here in the basilica, were used to decorate the covered colonnades surrounding gardens. This mask represents Medusa, one of the mythical Gorgon sisters, who had snakes for hair and who turned those who looked upon her to stone.

Fig. 140. ▷ ▷
Leptis Magna, Libya. Garden colonnade in which the columns are raised on a continuous dwarf wall anticipates the arrangement in the medieval cloister (see fig. 164).

Fig. 138.
Fresco from Leptis Magna, Libya. This painting shows a colonnaded villa on the banks of a Nile-like river teeming with scenes of everyday life. On the upper right side is a narrow planting bed that acts as a "green plinth" to the building beyond.

Many African gardens compare closely in plan and detail with those on the Italian mainland. The fountains and mosaic-floored colonnades of the garden courts in the excavated city of Volubilis (located in present-day Morocco) are difficult to separate in one's mind from garden courts elsewhere in the empire (figs. 141–44). However, adaptations to the standard Roman garden plan were made in response to the region's hot climate. For example, a feature of some African garden courts was the great size of the water storage cisterns constructed underneath, which enabled a substantial amount of water to be trapped and stored during the short rainy season (in some parts of Libya, rain falls for only a few days each year). This water reserve could then be drawn upon year-round for use in both house and garden.

The most remarkable adaptation to the climate of North Africa can be seen in the inland town of Bulla Regia, in present-day Tunisia. The houses had two floors, one at ground level and the other underground. The underground rooms were insulated from the intense summer heat. The courtyard at the heart of the house also had two stories, one of them underground. These courtyards enjoyed deep shade, which protected plants from drying out in the heat.

Other features were designed to combat the region's dry climate. Raised planting beds were sometimes used so that their stone or concrete edgings would confine irrigation water to the plants for which it was intended. A similar result was achieved by sinking the planting beds below the level of the surrounding walkways. The beds in the garden of the house known as Domus

Fig. 141.
House in Volubilis, Morocco. The horseshoe-shaped pool in this colonnaded courtyard reflected the increasing complexity of the architectural forms used in the late imperial period.

Fig. 142. ▽
House in Volubilis, Morocco. This spirally fluted column characterizes the sophistication of Roman decoration in the third century A.D. and anticipates the columns that pervaded the architecture and design of the succeeding Byzantine period.

Fig. 143. △
The House of Orpheus, Volubilis, Morocco. The remains of a colonnaded courtyard and a pool show a mosaic of Amphitrite located between the pool and the main reception room of the house (see fig. 144).

Fig. 144. ◁
The House of Orpheus, Volubilis, Morocco. A detail of the mosaic in fig. 143 shows Amphitrite in a chariot drawn by sea horses and surrounded by other sea creatures. When it was difficult in a dry climate to provide sufficient water for large ornamental pools, mosaics with a marine theme sometimes served as an acceptable substitute.

Sollectiana, at El Djem in Tunisia, appear to be sunk two-and-a-half feet below the level of the garden's surrounding covered colonnades. In some gardens, such as those of Thuburbo Majus in Tunisia, after water was used in the pools and fountains, it was run out from the garden through underground pipes and subsequently used to irrigate the crops in the surrounding fields.

The choice of planting for an African garden was dictated by the region's dry climate, in which it was difficult to grow many annual and perennial plants successfully. Instead, reliance on bulbs, trees, and shrubs for ornamental planting was pronounced. The date palm, with its distinctive silhouette, was to become the signature tree of the African garden. However, Italian cypresses, plane trees, and umbrella pine trees, typical of gardens on the Italian mainland, were shown planted around houses in African mosaics. Also shown in mosaics were pomegranates. These were referred to by the Romans as "Punic apples," that is, from the area of Carthage in North Africa.

Artichokes (*Cynara scolymus*) and marrows (*Cucurbita* sp.) are depicted as well and must have

been staples of African kitchen gardens. African marigolds (*Tagetes erecta*) were wild but pretty enough, perhaps, to be transplanted into a garden.

Many African mosaics of the second and third centuries A.D. depict scenes from everyday life, including that of the rural villa (figs. 145–51). From these depictions, it would appear that African country villas were generally two stories in height, the principal rooms being on the upper floor. Many of the villas seem to have had spacious open arcades along the front of the upper floor, which perhaps were decorated with potted plants. These structures are noteworthy in that most Roman villas elsewhere had flat-roofed colonnades on the ground floor, rather than such loggias with arched openings on an upper floor. The often remote locations of African villas may have dictated this arrangement for better security and protection. Some villas are shown with corner towers, the breezy upper rooms of which would have been used for relaxing during periods of summer heat (fig. 152); they would also have acted as lookout towers, enabling the occupants to scan the horizon for danger. The desire for

Fig. 145.
Mosaic from Thuburbo Majus, Tunisia, in the Bardo Museum, Tunis. Framed in a laurel scroll, this medallion represents Flora, the goddess of flowers and gardens.

Fig. 146.
Mosaic from Thuburbo Majus, Tunisia, in the Bardo Museum, Tunis. Ariadne reclines with Dionysus, the god of wine, who holds a twin-handled wine cup in his hand, in a work that illustrates the use of vine arbors to shade outdoor living spaces.

Fig. 147. △
Mosaic from Carthage, in the Bardo Museum, Tunis. This work illustrates a country villa entered through a colonnade. Behind are tall evergreen cypresses and deciduous trees, perhaps oriental planes. Their branches have been heavily cropped for firewood or for construction purposes, as was typical at that time.

Fig. 148. △
Mosaic from Carthage, in the Bardo Museum, Tunis. This leopard's setting of a pomegranate orchard suggests that he is part of a rich man's menagerie.

Fig. 149. ▽
Mosaic from Carthage, in the Bardo Museum, Tunis. Fishing scenes such as this took place not only in natural rivers and the sea but also in artificially stocked fishponds in large parks. Mosaics with an aquatic theme often formed the floors of decorative pools, their colors made brighter by the water playing over them.

Fig. 150. △
Mosaic from El Alia, Tunisia, in the Bardo Museum, Tunis.
A pair of globe artichokes (*Cynara scolymus*), a plant for
which Carthage was well known, is depicted here in
reverse symmetry. A variety of small, stylized, flowering
plants are illustrated in the margins of this mosaic.

Fig. 151. △
Mosaic from Oudna, Tunisia, in the Bardo Museum, Tunis.
This mosaic depicts grapevines twining on tall millet stalks
(*Sorghum vulgare*) growing out of pedestal urns.

Fig. 152. ◁
Mosaic from Tabarka, Tunisia, in the Bardo Museum,
Tunis. This country mansion, its upper loggia stretching
between twin towers, is set in the middle of a park full of
flowers and trees, including olives (*Olea europaea*) and
pomegranates. Birds, including pheasants, doves, ducks,
and thrushes, are splashing in the waters of a stream that
irrigates the property.

protection may have resulted in the walls of the villas having castle-like tops. Enclosures, the walls of which were also shown with battlemented tops, surrounded the villa (fig. 153). Depictions of these walls show them containing olive groves and vineyards (see fig. 152). The vines were often shown growing on unusual decorative metal supports in the form of large open cylinders or stakes (see figs. 151, 153). Mosaics also illustrate domestic and exotic fowl that roamed the gardens, as well as articles used by gardeners (figs. 154, 155; see also fig. 152).

Fig. 153. ▷
Mosaic from Tabarka, Tunisia, in the Bardo Museum, Tunis. Logically spaced and well-aligned vines on this country estate are pruned, dressed, and hoop-supported. The interspersed trees appear to be apples or quinces (*Cydonia oblonga*). The enclosing wall with battlements is depicted in front of the villa.

Fig. 154. ▷
Mosaic in the Bardo Museum, Tunis. A twin-handled basket typically used in gardens for carrying seedlings, flowers, fruit, and manure, made of wicker in a lattice weave.

Fig. 155. ▷ ▷
Mosaic in the Bardo Museum, Tunis. A peacock, a native Indian bird, and therefore an exotic in North Africa, prances in a vineyard.

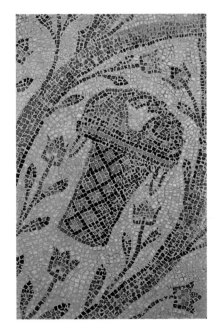

Fig. 156.
The House of the Water Jets, Conimbriga. When one entered this villa, an axial perspective opened up across the pool and reached as far as the villa's principal reception room, which was located beyond the furthest colonnade.

IBERIA

Iberia, which comprised present-day Spain and Portugal, became Rome's first continental province in the second century B.C. It was of particular significance for Rome as a rich source of minerals (silver, copper, tin, lead, and gold). The province also provided Rome with five emperors, including Trajan and Hadrian, and was the birthplace of such famous authors as Martial and Columella. Many of the region's native plants were described by Pliny the Elder and by the geographer Strabo (ca. 63 B.C.–ca. A.D. 23).

Most surviving Roman monuments in Spain are remnants of large public structures such as aqueducts and theaters. However, some domestic gardens have been excavated in the important Roman cities of Italica, Mérida, and Conimbriga, the latter in present-day Portugal. These gardens are valuable to us for the information they provide not only about Iberian gardens of the period, but also about gardens of the late imperial period in general. In the late second and the third centuries A.D., many Roman gardens were composed using complex rather than simple geometric forms, such as curves and countercurves. Another distinctive feature of these gardens is the inventive use of pools and fountains. In some gardens, a pool occupies almost the entire extent of a court, the planting beds being reduced to islands in the pool (figs. 156, 157).

Fig. 157.
The House of the Water Jets, Conimbriga. The larger courtyard in this villa was surrounded by colonnades with mosaic floors. The center of the courtyard was occupied by a great pool in which six formal planting beds formed islands of vegetation that were surrounded by a narrow perimeter rill.

Italica, near Seville in southwest Spain, was the birthplace of the emperors Hadrian and Trajan. It boasted luxurious houses and gardens, a number of which have been excavated. The garden of the House of the Birds is a typical example. The principal features of its colonnaded main courtyard were a pair of wellheads used to draw water from a cistern underneath. A pair of subsidiary courtyards lay at the rear. One was designed around a deep swimming or plunge pool, which was reached down a flight of steps. The other courtyard had a distinctively designed ornamental pool, its simple rectilinear shape varied by peripheral indents, alternately rectilinear and curvilinear. A pool in a garden at the nearby House of the Exedra was even more elaborate in design: its perimeter featured alternately curving and countercurving forms.

Mérida, in western Spain, contains more important Roman remains than any other Spanish town. The courtyard gardens in Mérida, like those of Italica, are distinguished by the inventiveness of their pool designs. The pool at the House of Mithras was in the form of a continuous narrow water channel running around the periphery of its courtyard. This ingenious configuration allowed the water in the channel to be replenished directly by rainwater running off the eaves of the roofs. A garden at the House of the Amphitheater has a similar peripheral channel in its courtyard that runs around only three sides. The effect of such a channel is to isolate a garden on an island in the middle of a courtyard—an interesting and unusual design conceit.

Fig. 158.
The House of the Swastikas, Conimbriga. An oblique view of this villa's central courtyard looks onto four formal planting beds set into the pool. The beds are quadrants made into two pairs by low semicircular walls.

Fig. 159.
The House of the Swastikas, Conimbriga. Among the famous geometric mosaics of Conimbriga is this example, a variant of the conventional swastika.

The gardens in the excavated Roman town of Conimbriga are also characterized by an imaginative use of water in their designs. Three courtyard gardens were planned with peripheral canals similar to those at Mérida, but this basic plan developed a number of variations. At the House of the Swastikas, the canal is augmented by two other narrow canals, one on the main axis and the other on the cross axis. This has the effect of creating four islands instead of one (figs. 158, 159). In the garden of the House of the Water Jets, the peripheral canal is supplemented by three canals dividing the garden into six islands rather than four (see fig. 157). Each individual island features decorative semicircular indents around its perimeter. The garden is further enlivened by the sight and sound of more than four hundred

separate water jets. The colonnade surrounding the garden has richly decorative mosaic floors in elaborate patterns. This garden, in spite of its remote provincial location, must have borne comparison in complexity of plan and refinement of detail with any garden of similar size found in Italy itself (fig. 160).

Fig. 160.
The House of the Water Jets, Conimbriga The villa boasted at least two courtyard gardens, the smaller of which is shown here. It has colonnades on three sides, the fourth side being formed by the boundary wall of the villa. A reflecting pool with a central fountain jet occupied the center.

GAUL

The Roman province of Gaul comprised an area including present-day France, Belgium, and the part of Germany that lies west of the Rhine River. For the purposes of garden history, it is convenient to divide the province into southern and northern Gaul.

The Mediterranean coastline of southern Gaul had a long history of settlement by the Greeks, which was followed by a period of long-standing alliance with Rome. Gallic textiles, glass, pottery, bronze, and iron contributed greatly to the Roman economy. It is not surprising that Roman culture influenced Gaul in return. In their style and decoration, the houses and gardens of Gaul began to follow typical Roman models. In the Roman town of Vaison, near the present-day city of Orange, an excavated house known as the House of the Silver Bust had a typical Roman-style atrium with two colonnaded court-yards beyond it. Each of the latter courtyards was planned around an open pool or plunge bath. Not far away, near the present-day town of Saint-Rémy-de-Provence, lies the excavated Roman town of Glanum. Here, the House of Artis had an atrium over an underground storage cistern, and a decorative shrine or altar was incorporated within the courtyard design. An extensive group of similar garden courtyards has been excavated at the Roman town of Saint-Roman-en-Gal, now a suburb of the city of Vienne. Many of these sites exhibit the complexity of design typical of late imperial gardens. They boast pools and fountains in a series of playful, not to say whimsical, designs including one with an arrangement of garden islands surrounded by peripheral canals similar to those of the Iberian gardens.

In addition, two important rural villas have been excavated that give us a sense of the Roman country garden in Gaul. They are both located close to the mountains of the Pyrenees in south-west France and both take advantage of the large sites that were usually available for country gardens. The Chiragan villa was begun in the Augustan age as a simple mansion laid out around a colonnaded court. It was enlarged during Trajan's reign by a garden court surrounded not by a continuous colonnade but by a vaulted corridor, which was extended outward at one point to give covered access to a small hexagonal summerhouse overlooking the Garonne River. The third period in the villa's history, from circa A.D. 150 to 200, saw the creation of a new fountain court built with local Pyrenean marble. Nearby, the great late imperial villa of Montmaurin was accessed down a long carriage drive. The villa's large ten-acre site was used to create an extensive semicircular entrance court. At the heart of the villa lay two successive colonnaded courtyards, the second boasting semicircular extensions on either side and a summerhouse at the rear. The extensive use of marble veneering on the villa's walls, together with aquariums for the display of ornamental fish, added to the luxuriant atmosphere. However, the villa lay in the path of marauding vandal tribes as they made their way through southwestern France to Spain. They reduced it to a ruin in the early fifth century.

Northern Gaul was little influenced by the Romans until its conquest by Julius Caesar in the middle of the first century B.C. Afterward, retired Roman soldiers were rewarded by Caesar with lands in Gaul, and Roman civil and military order was introduced. Gradually, Roman culture became preeminent.

The most interesting set of Roman gardens in northern Gaul was located near the city of Trier in present-day Germany. Located on the Moselle River, a tributary of the Rhine, Trier's importance dates from the third century A.D. When Diocletian divided the Roman Empire into four administrative units called tetrarchies, he made Trier one of the new capitals. As a result, many extensive riverside villas and gardens were laid out in the region during this period.

The rooms of a villa excavated at Nennig were arranged conventionally around courtyards with fountains. However, the villa also featured a terraced garden descending from a long portico to the riverbank as well as a sculpture-lined covered corridor leading to a detached bath-house. Some of the villas in the region were distinctively U-shaped in plan, their arms enclosing long riverside porticoes and terraces decorated with fountains and pools. The garden of a villa excavated at the present-day town of Welschbillig featured a pool measuring 190 feet long and 60 feet wide. It was large enough to allow for water sports and other staged entertainment such as the mock naval battles called "naumachiae," which were popular in Rome. In contrast, a garden excavated at Cologne, which is located further north on the banks of the Rhine, has revealed details of a relatively simple planting. It consisted of a vegetable plot, a separate orchard, a small oak grove, some open grassy spaces, and a pool shaded by three alder trees (*Alnus* sp.).

A general picture of life in the villas of Gaul is given in the eloquent writings of Ausonius (ca. A.D. 310–393) and Sidonius Apollinaris (ca. A.D. 465). Ausonius, in particular, had an eye for the rural villa set in the exhilarating natural landscape of the region. However, more detailed site excavations are needed if a clearer picture of the gardens of Roman Gaul is to emerge.

BRITAIN

Britain was invaded and overrun by the Romans in the middle of the first century A.D. As happened elsewhere, the conquerors established a settled administration that allowed commerce to develop. The Romans also introduced new agricultural crops and techniques. Gradually large houses with gardens were built both in the cities and in the country.

Our knowledge of Roman gardens in Britain is dominated by the thorough excavation that has taken place at the great country palace of Fishbourne, located near the present-day town of Chichester. In the first century A.D., the villa was among the largest in Europe outside Italy. The total grounds covered an area of about ten acres, the principal building consisting of four 200-foot-long colonnaded ranges enclosing a great courtyard. Within the courtyard a formal garden was laid out. On either side of the garden's central axis, a pair of long planting beds has been discovered during excavation. The most remarkable feature of these beds is that they were not straight but indented in form, the indents being alternately curvilinear and rectilinear along their length (fig. 161). This motif of alternating indent-

ed shapes is found repeatedly in Roman architectural and decorative design. After excavation,
these beds were planted with carefully trimmed
box hedging so that their precise form continues
to be evident. In addition to this main garden,
there were two smaller gardens, one to the north
and one to the south of the villa. It is thought
that one had a formal design while the other, that
facing the sea, had some informal elements.

A Roman city palace excavated on the banks
of the Thames River in London has a series of
riverside pools, which are thought to have been
part of the garden of the Roman governor of
Britain. More plentiful are the gardens of modest
rural villas that have been uncovered in other
parts of Britain. Examples include a villa garden
from the fourth century A.D. at Frocester Court
in Gloucestershire. Five separate planting beds
have been discovered lining an avenue that led to
a gravel sweep in front of the villa. The remains
of a formally planted grove of trees have also
been uncovered there. At a villa in Latymer in
Buckinghamshire, a terrace paved with rectilinear
stone slabs fronting the villa's portico and a
formal fishpond within an internal court have
been discovered.

In general, the cool, wet climate of Britain
engendered distinctive garden design features that
were not present in gardens on the European
mainland. For example, free-draining gravel,
rather than the sand or compacted earth found
on the continent, was used to surface driveways
and garden pathways. In the damp climate, planting played a greater role in gardens than it did
in the drier Mediterranean region. Lastly, the
columns of the peristyles were sometimes linked
by low intermediary walls as a protection against
wind and rain, a precaution unnecessary in
Mediterranean gardens.

The influence of the city of Rome waned
during the late imperial period. By the end of
the second century A.D., Rome's preeminent
status was lost and it became just one of many
resplendent cities of the empire. In contrast,
many provincial cities grew in wealth, power,
and splendor, as evidenced by the sophistication
of their gardens.

Fig. 161.
Fishbourne, England. Excavations at a city palace in
this Roman town have uncovered an extensive courtyard
garden, its broad central path leading from the original
entrance hall directly to the main reception hall. Excavations further revealed planting trenches on either side of
the path in a pattern of alternate semicircular and rectangular recesses strongly reminiscent of garden designs
illustrated in the wall-paintings of Herculaneum, except
that in the latter the plan is defined by trellis fences rather
than by box hedges.

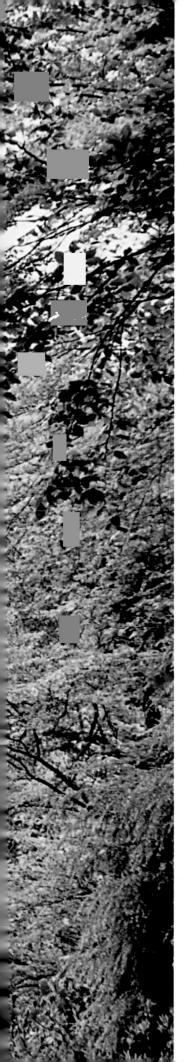

IV

THE INFLUENCE OF ROMAN GARDENS:
FROM BYZANTIUM TO THE TWENTIETH CENTURY

THE INFLUENCE OF Roman garden design has been continuous for nearly two thousand years and has been exerted in a number of ways and been apparent in many forms. During some periods of post-Roman history, the impact of this art form has been weaker and less direct than during others, but it has always returned in a subsequent period with renewed strength and in a more direct way.

Stourhead Garden, Wiltshire, England. In the eighteenth century, a simulated classical landscape, sometimes based on the paintings of the Roman Campagna by Claude Lorrain (1600–1682), was the preferred setting for classically inspired architecture. The design of this circular and domed Temple of Apollo was derived from the Temple of Venus at Baalbek (in present-day Lebanon), of which the antiquarian Richard Wood had published drawings in England in 1757. (See also fig. 167.)

BYZANTIUM

Rome's importance continued to decline during the latter half of the third century A.D. In 330, when the Roman Empire still extended over most of Europe, North Africa, and the Near East, the emperor Constantine (r. A.D. 306–337) formally moved the capital from Rome to Byzantium, which he renamed Constantinople (now Istanbul). In succeeding centuries the western part of the empire (present-day western Europe) gradually fell asunder, but the Eastern Empire, known as the Byzantine Empire, continued as a major power for more than one thousand years, ending only with the fall of Constantinople in 1453.

The Byzantine Empire boasted an important garden tradition, but none of its gardens survive in their entirety or none has been extensively excavated. What we know of its gardens derives from depictions of them, or of elements from them, in mosaics and frescoes. Gardens were seldom the main subjects of Byzantine art, which confines itself almost exclusively to Christian themes. However, some biblical events were set in gardens, so artists provided garden backgrounds in those depictions. Byzantine images of the Garden of Eden or of the Annunciation thus provide us with information about the Byzantine concept of a garden. Sometimes artists chose to portray saints or other holy men in a garden setting, in works that also provide us with precious details of the gardens of the time.

Gardens enclosed by decorative architectural screens are shown in many Byzantine frescoes. Some frescoes depict open colonnades or arcades dividing and defining individual garden areas. These colonnades can be so elaborate that they rival the fanciful garden colonnades seen in Roman architectural paintings of the first century B.C. In some Byzantine paintings, a figure or a group of figures is set against the backdrop of a single open-air canopied pavilion, providing a clue as to what real garden pavilions must have looked like in Byzantine times.

Various kinds of fountain basins are shown. Raised fountain basins veneered with colorful marble as well as urn and bowl fountains, the latter based closely on Roman models, are numerous in frescoes, mosaics, and illuminated manuscripts (fig. 162). One might be forgiven for thinking that the decorative garden fencing shown in some Byzantine frescoes is in fact Roman, so close is the resemblance in style. Plants such as the cypress, the ivy, and the vine as well as wildflowers such as the Madonna lily grace frescoes and the bas-relief carvings in stone, ivory, and wood so characteristic of Byzantine art. Exotic birds such as pheasants and peacocks are depicted strutting in garden settings. All of these images can be found in frescoes of Roman gardens and are evidence of the close relationship between the two imperial garden styles.

THE ISLAMIC GARDEN

Roman influences on the gardening traditions of Islam were more indirect since they were transmitted through Byzantium. Many of the great classical texts of ancient Greece and Rome were translated into Arabic between the eighth and the twelfth centuries. Among these were technical texts that formed the basis for the rapid development of Arabic science and engineering. In particular, the study of hydraulics as developed by Hero of Alexandria, the Greek writer and scientist from the first century A.D., formed the basis for Arabic hydraulics, which in turn played a vital role in the development of the large-scale irrigation works that made much of the dry lands of the Near East more fertile.

Hydraulics contributed to the development of the Islamic garden by making possible the construction of increasingly complex garden pools, canals, and fountains. The fountains at the royal court of Damascus (in present-day Syria) were renowned for their automatons, or moving parts. These included bronze birds that were made to "sing" as water at different pressures passed through them.

The basic Islamic courtyard house was derived from that of the Romans. Just as the Roman peristyle garden was surrounded by a continuous covered colonnade, the Islamic courtyard featured a covered arcade (fig. 163). And just as the Roman courtyard garden focused on a pool or fountain and was planted with shade trees, the later Islamic courtyard was similarly watered and shaded. The use of potted plants was characteristic of both. Many additional minor features and details of Islamic garden design can likewise be traced to Roman examples.

Fig. 162. ◁
Mosaic from the Church of San Vitale, Ravenna. This sixth-century mosaic shows Empress Theodora and her retinue standing by a pedestaled bowl fountain modeled on those featured in the gardens of classical Rome.

Fig. 163. ▷
Court of the Lions, Alhambra, Spain. Alhambra, the palace of the Moorish kingdom of Granada, includes the supreme example of Arabic gardens from the thirteenth and fourteenth centuries. Taking advantage of water from the nearby Sierra Nevada, the gardens and courtyards of the palace display a profusion of water in fountains and pools. The central fountain in the Court of the Lions is fed by water flowing through shallow channels from each of the four sides of the courtyard. The surrounding colonnade is reminiscent of the peristyles of Roman gardens.

THE MIDDLE AGES

The cloister gardens of the medieval monasteries of western Europe derived their general arrangement from the classical garden court. Although vandal tribes destroyed much of the Roman Empire in the west, Roman civilization lived on in the Eastern Empire, and the subsequent spread of monasticism from the east resulted in the foundation of the great western European monasteries. Through the contacts that the western monastic orders maintained with their eastern counterparts, classical Greece and Rome influenced medieval Europe, albeit indirectly.

The classical Roman peristyle reappeared on a much larger scale in the medieval cloister garden (fig. 164). The medieval courtyard, following the Roman model, was surrounded by a continuous covered vaulted corridor, which then became known as the "cloister." As in Roman examples, the medieval cloister garden comprised a planting of shade trees with a pool, well, or fountain. Although there is little resemblance in the architectural detail between the Roman courtyard and the medieval cloister, the underlying conception and form, as well as the incorporation of water and planting into the courtyard interiors, are similar.

The legacy of classical gardening prevailed on a more practical level as well through the medieval period in western Europe. Pliny's *Natural History* and the works of Varro, Columella, and Palladius were still in active use and had not been supplanted by any medieval texts. Palladius's book was particularly valued for his method of imparting hints on what to do during each month of the year, in "gardener's calendar" form. Furthermore, we know from illustrations in medieval illuminated books that topiary—the garden craft invented by the Romans—continued to be popular, gracing many of the small, enclosed castle gardens of the period.

Fig. 164.
The cloister of the cathedral of Monreale, Sicily. As seen in this twelfth-century cathedral, the concept of the medieval cloister garden derives from the Roman peristyle garden.

THE RENAISSANCE

While the garden traditions of Islam and of medieval Europe were influenced indirectly by Roman traditions, those of Renaissance Europe were under a much more direct influence. In the fifteenth century, Europe began to look for inspiration in the texts and artifacts that had survived, often in a fragmentary state, from the classical Greek and Roman periods. This revival of interest in classical culture and the subsequent period of artistic endeavor became known as the Renaissance. At the time, the buildings of ancient Rome were in better condition than they are today, and the decorations and artifacts of these structures and their gardens were more visible. Aspiring architects and designers in Renaissance Rome spent their apprenticeship measuring, drawing, and learning from these remains, although the drawings they produced varied from precise copies to designs that added highly personal embellishments to the original structures.

This new interest in the classical period resulted in a fashion of creating gardens with views over the ruins of the ancient city. The Renaissance painter Raphael (1483–1520) was part of a cultured circle that met in a garden overlooking the remains of the ancient Forum of Trajan. The great connoisseur pope Alessandro Farnese, Paul III, commissioned Vignola (1507–1573), the prime architect of his time in Rome, to design new gardens on the Palatine Hill, hallowed as the site of ancient Rome's imperial palace. The desire of artists and their patrons to associate themselves with the civilization of ancient Rome grew in intensity (fig. 165).

Most of the ancient Roman buildings still standing in the Renaissance period were those of a public nature and so were appropriately monumental in scale. It is not surprising therefore that the first Renaissance villas and gardens to be laid out following classical Roman models were conceived on a similarly massive scale. The famous terraces designed by the architect Bramante (1444–1514) to link the Vatican Palace in Rome with the Belvedere, a garden pavilion located on a hill a thousand feet away, were designed on an architectural scale unmatched in Europe in a

secular ornamental building since classical times. The terraced gardens of what is now known as the Villa Madama in Rome were designed by Raphael. Although only partly executed, what is seen today of the terraces' supporting walls indicates their intended grandeur. Bramante's pupil, the architect Baccio Bandinelli, introduced the monumentally scaled garden to Florence with his design for the Boboli Gardens, which were laid out behind the Pitti Palace for the Medici family.

Palladio (1508–1580), an architect from the Venetian region of Italy, also studied the ruins of classical Rome carefully. From them he took inspiration that was different from that taken by the Roman and Florentine architects. He was not impressed so much by the monumental scale of classical architecture as by the possibilities of transforming the idea of a classical temple into that of a house. This he succeeded in doing most memorably in his famous design for the Villa Rotunda outside Vicenza, a town on the Venetian mainland. Consistent with his concept of the house as temple, he did not surround it with a conventional garden but with a modified temple precinct. Simple arrangements of different ground levels delineated by low retaining walls, formal flights of steps, low hedges, and occasional votive urns or statuary—all elements used in traditional temple sanctuaries—still define the setting of the villa today.

Architects such as Palladio were able to use the new technology of printing to publish books of their survey drawings of Roman sites. They also sometimes produced books of their own designs for houses and gardens. A diverse range of authors such as the architect Sebastiano Serlio, the poet Francesco Colonna, the botanist P. A. Mattioli, and the engravers Lauro, Maggi, and

Fig. 165.
Villa d'Este in Tivoli, east of Rome. Tall cypresses and evergreen hedging flank the central walk of this Renaissance garden, which leads to grotto-like fountain niches similar to those found in the gardens of ancient Rome. See also fig. 184.

Falda all produced books with reproductions of gardens, garden designs, and plants. Through the distribution of such books, knowledge of classical garden design and planting was disseminated throughout Europe and, subsequently, to America. Thus, the inspiration of classical garden design spread worldwide (fig. 166).

The gardens of Renaissance Italy maintained another connection with the classical world in that some were conceived as settings for the great collections of antique sculpture gathered by connoisseurs in Rome during that period.

Bramante's terraces at the Vatican Palace featured numerous lateral niches specifically designed for life-size figures from the papal collection of antiquities. The gardens of the Villa Medici in Rome were conceived partly to display many of the pieces in the great Medici collection of antique sculpture. The external walls of the casino, or garden house, known as the Villa Pia in the Vatican gardens were designed to incorporate antique bas-reliefs, and the art of classical mosaic was revived to decorate the walls as well as the garden gates.

Fig. 166.
Early eighteenth-century plan of the urban garden of Palazzo Giusti in Verona. This Renaissance garden, created 1572–1583 and largely unchanged to this day, comprises a series of individual smaller gardens, which ultimately derive both in scale and design from the formal gardens of ancient Rome. From *Ville, giardini e paesaggi del Veneto nelle incisioni dell'opera di Johann Christoph Volkamer*, ed. Ennio Concina, intro. Lionello Puppi (1714; Milan: Edizioni Il Polifilo, 1979), p. LXXX.

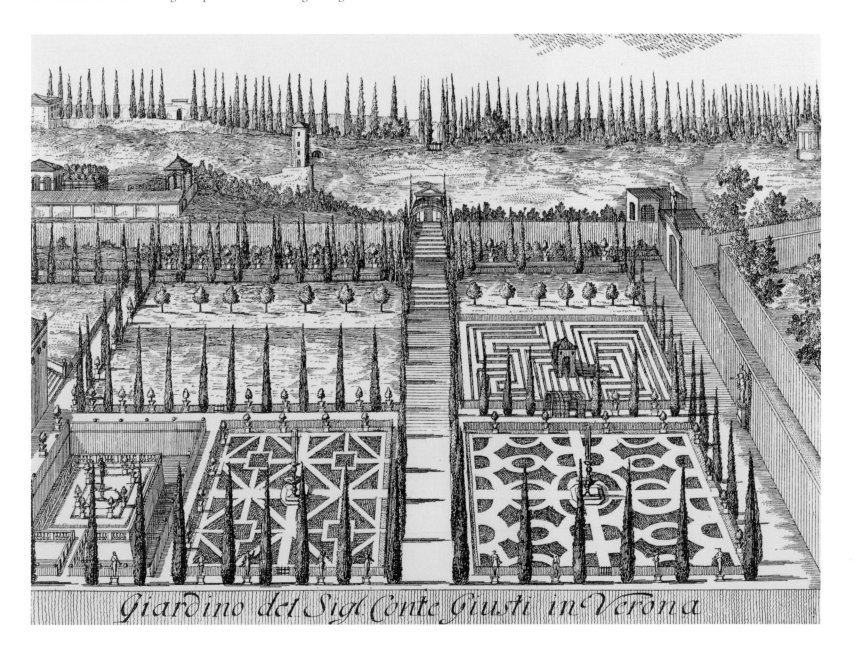

Giardino del Sig. Conte Giusti in Verona

THE BAROQUE

The experimentation with the forms of Renaissance architecture and garden design that characterized the Baroque in seventeenth-century Europe paralleled the experimentation with conventional classical forms that took place in the architecture and garden design of late imperial Rome. There was a similar interest in the development of more and more complex forms. Squares, circles, triangles, and rectangles—the geometry of classicism—were replaced during both the late Roman and the Baroque periods by polygons, ovals, curves, and countercurves. Broken and segmental rather than complete geometrical forms were preferred. Theatricality replaced restraint in design, marked by the lavish use of luxury materials, during each of these widely separated periods.

The curves and countercurves of garden pools in late Roman towns such as Italica in Spain anticipated the elaborate forms of the pool designed for the water parterre at Versailles by the French Baroque garden architect Le Nôtre (1613–1700). The alternately rectilinear and semicircular indents in the clipped hedges in the garden at Fishbourne (see fig. 161) are echoed in the similar indentation of a pool in the Baroque garden at the Villa Torlonia at Frascati near Rome. Although the connection between Baroque gardens and those of late imperial Rome has not been conclusively established, the resemblance in form is too close not to merit noting here.

THE LANDSCAPE GARDEN

By the beginning of the eighteenth century, the tradition of the formally planned symmetrical garden as a setting for a house was becoming exhausted. New inspiration for a building's setting was being sought in the landscape paintings of Claude Lorrain (1600–1682), Salvator Rosa (1615–1673), and their colleagues, who painted the countryside around Rome still littered with old temples and other classical ruins, as Rome itself was. The idea of a house of classically inspired architecture in a setting that approximated a landscape painting by Claude gained currency. Claude's landscapes were considered to have a special authenticity because he was seen as the successor to Studius, the originator of classical landscape painting in Rome during the age of Augustus. Although Studius and his school painted on walls rather than on canvas, their subject matter and their painting style were similar to those of Claude and his school. The ancient Roman school favored panoramic landscapes with informally grouped trees, springs, temples, country houses, rustic shrines, and statues. These paintings were populated by small groups of people such as worshipers, wayfarers, fishermen, and goatherds. Flocks of goats and sheep, as well as herds of cattle, were usually depicted. This description applies as well to a seventeenth-century landscape painting by Claude and to the idealized landscape gardens created around country houses by English gentlemen in the eighteenth century and later in other European countries and in America.

Just as the landscape paintings were filled with scattered temples, so these landscape gardens were scattered with ornamental park buildings. Small temples based on Roman models with names like the Temple of Flora or the Temple of Venus were favored. At the great English landscape garden of Stourhead, a small domed structure was named the Pantheon after its model in Rome (fig. 167). In the park at Wörlitz in Germany, a large mound of stones was raised in imitation of Vesuvius. On special occasions, a bonfire was lit in this miniature representation of the volcano so as to simulate an eruption. On its slope, a small "Italian cottage" was built and named the Villa Hamilton, in honor of the eighteenth-century British antiquarian Sir William Hamilton, a patron of the excavations of the classical ruins around Naples. In the royal park of Virginia Water at Surrey in England actual columns and other fragments from Leptis Magna, the Roman site in present-day Libya, were erected in 1826 to suggest a ruined temple.

NEOCLASSICISM

Another surge of interest in classical architecture and design occurred at the end of the eighteenth century. Architects of the time were inspired to produce a whole series of conjectural drawings of Pliny's villas and gardens based on the detailed descriptions of them surviving in his *Letters*. Architects from France, Germany, Spain, Italy, Poland, and England all created versions, each taking a different view of the grounds, but all bearing a family resemblance (see pp. 2–3).

A renewed archaeological interest resulted in the first systematic excavations of Hadrian's Villa at Tivoli and of the cities of Herculaneum and Pompeii. (The excavations in previous periods had been haphazard.) Subsequently, books containing engraved views of the excavated houses and gardens of Pompeii and Herculaneum by artists such as Jacob Philippe Hackaert (1737–1807), the brothers Fausto (1812?–1886) and Felice (b. 1816?) Niccolini, and others began to circulate and have a wide impact (see fig. 94). These engravings sometimes illustrated attempts by excavators to reconstruct the detailed garden layouts by reassembling the sculpture and other decorative objects found on the site and by restoring the planting of the gardens in a conjectural way. These images became widely available and inspired readers to emulate these reconstructed garden designs from ancient Rome in their own homes.

Another factor in the revival of ancient garden design during the Neoclassical period was the greater availability of copies of classical sculpture. During previous centuries, copies of ancient sculpture were produced solely for royalty and especially wealthy aristocrats. The great connoisseur kings of France, Francis I (r. 1515–1547) and Louis XIV (r. 1643–1715), ordered many such copies to place in their gardens. It was both expensive and difficult to arrange for full-size copies, usually carried out in bronze or marble. During the eighteenth century, cheaper copies in lead were sold by workshops such as that of John Cheare in London. However, mass production was only initiated at the beginning of the nineteenth century. The demand for less expensive copies was such that miniaturized versions of the great pieces were widely produced. Miniatures were ideal as ornaments in the smaller gardens of the less wealthy aristocrats, the gentry, and the middle classes.

Fig. 167.
Stourhead Garden, Wiltshire, England. Created in 1741–1765, this garden exemplifies a yearning for the Vergilian Arcady characterized by Neoclassical buildings set in a naturalistic landscape. The Temple of Apollo, seen here, along with further temples, statuary, and a grotto all contribute to the Arcadian illusion of the garden.

ECLECTICISM

Nineteenth-century gardens in Europe and America reflected many different stylistic influences mixed together in a variety of ways—a composite style known as "eclecticism." Although the influence of the gardens of ancient Rome is apparent in many gardens of this period, it is only one among many sources of inspiration. Examples of great nineteenth-century gardens incorporating areas influenced by Roman models include Sandringham in England, the Parc Monceau in Paris, and the Achilleion on the island of Corfu in Greece.

In the royal garden of Sandringham, a monumental semicircular stone seat forms a focal point. Its designer was Sir Lawrence Alma-Tadema (1836–1912), a Victorian painter who looked to ancient Greece and Rome for inspiration and included re-creations of classical gardens in his paintings. The garden seat at Sandringham is based closely on those he often depicted in his canvases.

The landscaped public park in Paris called Parc Monceau features a large pool partly surrounded by an open colonnade. The structure was called La Naumachie after the *naumachiae*, the large pools designed for water sports and entertainment that were popular in ancient Rome.

In 1890–1891, Empress Elizabeth of Austria (1837–1898) built a classically inspired palace on a hill overlooking the Mediterranean on Corfu, an island off present-day Greece. Called the Achilleion after Achilles, her classical hero, one of the palace's gardens was modeled on a Pompeian peristyle.

During the second half of the nineteenth century, the great Italian photography studios of Alinari and Brogi contributed to the more widespread appreciation of the houses and gardens of Pompeii and Herculaneum through the production and sale of albums of photographs depicting the excavated sites.

TWENTIETH CENTURY

At the turn of the twentieth century, there was a fashion for constructing villas along the Bay of Naples in the locations of ancient Roman sites. The attraction was the possibility of having some excavated or partly excavated classical ruins as one of the focal points of a villa's garden. This feature would give the garden a kind of instant history and an association with the classical world that was much prized.

On the island of Capri, a Swedish doctor and writer, Axel Munthe, bought the Villa San Michele in 1896. During the construction of the garden, the partial ruins of what is thought to be one of Tiberius's villas were found. These still form part of the garden's ornament today.

At Sorrento, Lord Astor, a former U.S. ambassador to Italy, bought a summer villa in 1905. He was delighted to discover a building on site that had belonged to Agrippa Posthumus (d. A.D. 14), son of the consul Agrippa. To enhance this

Fig. 168. ◁
Lord Astor's villa at Sorrento. In the early twentieth century, Lord Astor placed some of his archaeological collection in the villa's garden, transforming it into a treasure trove of antiquities. The antique column with a fluted shaft shown here has been made to serve as a support for an opening in the garden's boundary wall that offers a glimpse of the sea.

Fig. 169. ▷
Lord Astor's villa at Sorrento. White marble urn of antique *tazza* shape placed atop an Ionic capital, which in turn rests on part of a column shaft with a vine pattern, in an innovative use of assorted antique fragments.

association, Astor assembled in his garden a collection of antiquities from all periods but predominantly sculpture of the classical Roman age (figs. 168–73). When he returned to his place of principal residence, Hever Castle in Kent, England, Lord Astor created one area in his vast garden that he called the Pompeian Wall. The wall was constructed with a series of recesses that were crammed with the antique statues and fragments of Roman buildings he had collected. Subsequently, this part of the garden was lushly planted to create the effect of an area of ruined antiquity rapidly disappearing under the growth of rampant vegetation.

Fig. 170. ◁
Lord Astor's villa at Sorrento. Rather than display the full panorama of the Bay of Naples from his villa's garden, Lord Astor constructed a high wall along the garden's sea front. At intervals along its length, architecturally framed openings with tantalizing sea views were created. The tall bamboo screen above the wall is a modern, but traditionally built, wind shelter for the garden's tender plants.

Fig. 171. ◁
Lord Astor's villa at Sorrento. A white marble head of Mars placed on a tall plinth mimics an antique herm. To the left of the statue is a structure made of dry palm fronds, which acts as a shield for tender plants during inclement weather.

Fig. 172. ▷
Lord Astor's villa at Sorrento. Roman sarcophagus from the early Christian period adapted to stand on a pair of upturned Corinthian capitals in an arrangement known in architectural terms as a palimpsest, referring to the re-use of antique architectural elements in a new and unexpected setting. Note that the wall behind the sarcophagus has been built in a form of Roman stonework known as *opus reticulatum*, in which coursed stonework was laid diagonally.

Fig. 173. △
Lord Astor's villa at Sorrento. Adapted to a fluted
pedestal, this imposing statue of Neptune presides over
a water-lily pool. The background of large palms evokes
the exotic planting that might have characterized a garden
in Roman Africa.

Harold Peto (1854–1953), the renowned Arts and Crafts English garden designer, was also an inveterate collector of classical antiquities. His own garden at Iford Manor in Wiltshire became a virtual outdoor museum of historical artifacts. Among the many sections of his garden was an area known as the North Walk. It was decorated with groupings of Etruscan, Greek, and Roman objects. Peto designed gardens with similar collections of decorative antiquities for his clients. At the garden of Garinish Island off the coast of Ireland, he designed a paved court with a mosaic-lined pool reminiscent of Pompeian gardens. The tradition of building gardens in the Roman style using original antique fragments as decoration continues to this day, as seen in a recently created villa garden at Hammamet in Tunisia (figs. 174–78).

Fig. 174.
Hammamet, Tunisia. In this modern seaside villa near Tunis, the garden is decorated with antique Roman columns, column capitals and pedestals, and pools inspired by Roman models. The luxuriant vegetation reminds us that the ancient Roman garden featured a balance of stone architecture and ornament with rich planting.

Fig. 175.
Hammamet, Tunisia. Raised reflecting pools suggest
the water storage cisterns of ancient Rome. An antique
Corinthian column capital is raised above the water on
its own platform.

Fig. 176.
Hammamet, Tunisia. The garden's long canal focuses on another antique column shaft and is flanked by vegetation, its luxuriance echoing that depicted in many Roman garden frescoes.

Fig. 177.
Hammamet, Tunisia. The shafts of antique columns mark level changes, the pool beyond reflecting the blue Mediterranean sky and potted plants.

Fig. 178.
Hammamet, Tunisia. An antique
mosaic has been incorporated
into the floor of a path leading to
the Mediterranean Sea.

American enthusiasts for the classical world also boasted gardens with areas based on Roman models. Beginning in 1924, Louise du Pont Crowninshield, of the du Pont family of industrialists, created a ruined garden near Wilmington, Delaware, that was partly modeled on Roman antecedents. A section of publishing magnate William Randolph Hearst's eclectic garden at San Simeon in California, also dating from the 1920s, was designed in Neoclassical style and christened the Neptune Pool. However, these gardens boasted but partial reconstructions of Roman garden features. It was not until the 1970s, with oil industrialist and art collector J. Paul Getty's re-creation of the Villa dei Papiri of ancient Herculaneum in Malibu, California, that a comprehensive reconstruction of a complete Roman villa and garden was attempted (figs. 179–83).

Fig. 179. ◁
The J. Paul Getty Museum, Malibu, California. Built in the early 1970s, this museum is based on a plan of the Villa dei Papiri, a large, suburban villa just outside the town of Herculaneum on the Bay of Naples. Buried under some 30 m of pyroclastic mudflow in the eruption of Mt. Vesuvius in A.D. 79, the villa was rediscovered in 1750. The building was partially explored through underground tunnels, and a plan was drawn of the house and its impressive peristyle gardens and pools.

Fig. 180. ▷
The J. Paul Getty Museum, Malibu, California. The vegetation in the large peristyle garden consists of plants that are all known to have grown in Roman gardens. The topiary hedges and the trees and plants are laid out in patterns familiar from Roman frescos and excavated gardens.

Fig. 181. △
The J. Paul Getty Museum, Malibu, California. A peristyle encloses the large garden surrounding a pool. In the Villa dei Papiri, this pool may have been a large water reservoir—it had a capacity of some 225,000 gallons of water.

Fig. 182. ◁
The J. Paul Getty Museum, Malibu, California. A small courtyard garden has in its center a large fountain, whose basin overflows into a circular pool. Note the nymphaeum on the back wall, which is modeled on one in the House of the Grand Fountain (see fig. 22).

Fig. 183. ▷
The J. Paul Getty Museum, Malibu, California. The herb garden, on the outside of the large peristyle garden, is laid out in symmetrical beds around a central well. Fruit trees rise from beds of herbs such as thyme, rosemary, basil, lavender, and dusty miller. Olive trees are planted on terraces overlooking the herb garden. The Pacific Ocean is visible in the background.

SELECT LIST OF PLANTS GROWN IN ANCIENT ROMAN GARDENS

ACANTHUS • *Acanthus mollis*

AFRICAN MARIGOLD • *Tagetes erecta*

ALDER • *Alnus* sp.

ALEPPO PINE • *Pinus halepensis*

ALLIUM • *Allium* sp.

ALMOND • *Prunus dulcis*

APPLE • *Malus* sp.

APRICOT • *Prunus armeniaca*

ARTICHOKE • *Cynara scolymus*

ASPARAGUS • *Asparagus officinalis*

ASTER • *Aster* sp.

BASIL • *Basilicum* sp.

BAY LAUREL • *Laurus nobilis*

BLACKBERRY • *Rubus* sp.

BOX • *Buxus sempervirens*

BULLACE • *Prunus domestica*

BUTCHER'S BROOM • *Ruscus aculeata*

CABBAGE • *Brassica deracea*

CAEN ANEMONE • *Anemone coronaria*

CAMPANULA • *Campanula* sp.

CAROB • *Ceratonia siliqua*

CELERY • *Apium graveolens*

CHAMOMILE • *Chamaemelum nobile*

CHERRY • *Prunus cerasus* (EDIBLE CHERRY)

CHICKWEED • *Cerastium* sp.

CITRON • *Citrus medica*

CORIANDER • *Coriandrum sativum*

CORNEL • *Cornus mas*

CRAB APPLE • *Malus sylvestris*

CROCUS • *Crocus sativus*

CUCUMBER • *Cucumis sativus*

CYPRESS • *Cupressus sempervirens*

DAISY • *Bellis perennis*

DAMSON PLUM • *Prunus damascena*

DATE PALM • *Phoenix dactylifera*

DILL • *Anethum graveolens*

DUSTY MILLER • *Artemisia stelleriana*

ELM • *Ulmus campestris*

EVERGREEN (or "WINTER") OAK •
   Quercus ilex

FENNEL • *Foeniculum vulgare*

FENUGREEK • *Trigonella foenum-graecum*

FEVERFEW • *Chrysanthemum parthenium*

FIG • *Ficus carica*

FLAX • *Linum* sp.

FORGET-ME-NOT • *Myosotis arvensis*

GARLIC • *Allium sativum*

GLADIOLUS • *Gladiolus* sp.

GOLDEN PLUM • *Prunus italica*

GOURD • *Cucurbita* sp.

GRAPEVINE • *Vitis vinifera*

HART'S-TONGUE FERN • *Phyllitis scolopendrium*

HOLLOW-STEMMED BAMBOO •
   possibly *Arundo donax*

HOUND'S TONGUE • *Cynoglossum officinale*

HYACINTH • *Hyacinthus orientalis*

IRIS • *Iris* sp.

IVY • *Hedera* sp.

JUJUBE • *Zizyphus jujube*

JUNIPER • *Juniperus communis*

KIDNEY VETCH • *Anthyllis vulneraria*

LARKSPUR • *Delphinium* sp.

LAUREL • *Prunus laurocerasus*

LAUREL ROSE • *Cistus laurifolius*

LAURUSTINUS • *Viburnum tinus*

LAVENDER • *Lavandula* sp.

LEEK • *Allium ampeloprasum*

LEMON • *Citrus limon*

LINDEN • *Tilia* sp.

LYCHNIS • *Lychnis* sp.

MADONNA LILY • *Lilium candidum*

MAIDENHAIR FERN • *Adiantum pedatum*

MALLOW • *Malva sylvestris*

MARIGOLD • *Calendula officinalis*

MARROW • *Cucurbita* sp.

MARTAGON LILY • *Lilium martagon*

MEDLAR • *Mespilus germanica*

MELON • *Cucumis melo*

MILLET • *Sorghum vulgare*

MORNING GLORY • *Ipomoea* sp.

Fig. 184.
Villa d'Este, Tivoli. In this Renaissance garden, a fountain known as the *Rometta*, or Little Rome, was created to represent in miniature the ancient city of Rome and its principal monuments, waterworks, and fountains. In front of the fountain flows a stream representing the Tiber river with a boat-shaped island simulating the Tiber Island.

MULBERRY · *Morus nigra*

MUSTARD · *Brassica negra*

MYRTLE · *Myrtus communis*

NARCISSUS · *Narcissus* sp.

NETTLE TREE · *Celtis australis*

OLEANDER · *Nerium oleander*

OLIVE · *Olea europaea*

ONION · *Allium cepa*

OPIUM POPPY · *Papaver somniferum*

ORACHE · *Atriplex hortensis*

ORANGE · *Citrus aurantium*

ORIENTAL PLANE TREE · *Platanus orientalis*

PALE YELLOW KIDNEY VETCH ·
    Anthyllis vulneraria

PARSLEY · *Petroselinum crispum*

PARSNIP · *Pastinaca sativa*

PEACH · *Prunus persica*

PEAR · *Pyrus communis*

PERIWINKLE · *Vinca minor*

PINE · *Pinus* sp.

PINK · *Dianthus* sp.

PLANTAIN · *Plantago* sp.

POMEGRANATE · *Punica granatum*

POPPY · *Papaver rhoeas*

PURPLE PLUM · *Prunus domestica*

PURPLE VIOLET · *Viola odorata*

QUINCE · *Cydonia oblonga*

RADISH · *Raphanus sativus*

RASPBERRY · *Rubus idaeus*

ROCKET · *Hesperis matronalis*

ROSE · *Rosa* sp.

ROSE OF CYRENE · possibly *Rosa sempervirens*

ROSE OF PAESTUM · *Rosa x damascena "Bifera"*

ROSE OF PRAENESTE · possibly *Rosa gallica
    centifolia*

ROSEMARY · *Rosmarinus officinalis*

SAMPHIRE · *Crithmum maritimum*

SCILLA · *Scilla* sp.

SERVICEBERRY · *Sorbus domestica*

SMILAX · *Smilax aspera*

STONE PINE · *Pinus pinea*

STRAWBERRY · *Fragaria* sp.

STRAWBERRY TREE · *Arbutus unedo*

SWEET CHESTNUT · *Castanea sativa*

THYME · *Thymus* sp.

TURNIP · *Brassica campestris*

UMBRELLA PINE · *Pinus pinea*

VERVAIN · *Verbena officinalis*

WALNUT · *Juglans regia*

WHITE LILY · *Lilium candidum*

WHITE POPLAR · *Populus alba*

WILD CHRYSANTHEMUM · *Chrysanthemum* sp.

WILD STRAWBERRY · *Fragaria vesca*

YELLOW VIOLET · *Viola lutea*

PHOTO CREDITS

Patrick Bowe: fig. 184.

e. t. archive, Nicolas Sapieha: title page, figs. 17, 18, 33, 124, 168–73.

Alfredo e Pio Foglia, Naples: half-title page, p. iv, p. ix upper left, figs. 1, 4–7, 12, 13, 15, 20–24, 26–32, 34–59, 61, 80–110, 120.

Getty Research Institute, Research Library, Los Angeles: p. 2, fig. 166.

Benedicte Gilman: fig. 165.

Nils Gilman: fig. 163.

Kurt Hauser: fig. 167.

MBAC—Soprintendenza Archeologica di Roma: fig. 60.

© Scala/Art Resource, NY: p. ix lower right, figs. 162, 164.

Julius Shulman: figs. 179–82.

Mark Edward Smith, Venice: p. ix upper right and lower left, p. 110, p. 170, figs. 2, 3, 10, 11, 14, 62–79, 111–19, 121–23, 125–40, 145–60, 174–78.

Soprintendenza per i Beni Archeologici delle province di Napoli e Caserta: figs. 8, 9, 16, 19, 25.

Lisa Train: figs. 141–44, 161.

Alexander Vertikoff: p. 169, fig. 183.

SUGGESTIONS FOR FURTHER READING

Carroll, Maureen. *Earthly Paradises: Ancient Gardens in History and Archaeology.* Los Angeles, 2003.

Cunliffe, Barry. *Fishbourne: A Roman Palace and Its Garden.* London, 1971.

Farrar, Linda. *Gardens of Italy and the Western Provinces of the Roman Empire: From the Fourth Century B.C. to the Fourth Century A.D.* Oxford, 1996.

Farrar, Linda. *Ancient Roman Gardens.* Phoenix Mill, Thrupp, Stroud, Gloustershire, 1998.

Gabriel, Mabel M. *Livia's Garden Room at Prima Porta.* New York, 1955.

Gunther, Robert T. *The Greek Herbal of Dioscorides.* New York, 1959.

Hunt, John Dixon, ed. *Garden History: Issues, Approaches, Methods.* Dumbarton Oaks Colloquium on the History of Landscape Architecture, vol. 13. Washington, D.C., 1992.

Jashemski, Wilhelmina Feemster. *The Gardens of Pompeii: Herculaneum and the Villas Destroyed by Vesuvius.* Vols. 1–2. New Rochelle, NY, 1979–1993.

MacDonald, William L., and John A. Pinto. *Hadrian's Villa and Its Legacy.* New Haven, 1995.

MacDougall, Elisabeth B., ed. *Ancient Roman Villa Gardens.* Dumbarton Oaks Colloquium on the History of Landscape Architecture, vol. 10. Washington, D.C., 1987.

MacDougall, Elisabeth B., and Wilhelmina F. Jashemski, eds. *Ancient Roman Gardens.* Dumbarton Oaks Colloquium on the History of Landscape Architecture, vol. 7. Washington, D.C., 1981.

Pliny the Elder. *Natural History.* Trans. H. Rackham. Loeb Classical Library. Cambridge, MA, 1952.

Pliny the Younger. *Epistles.* Trans. B. Radice. Loeb Classical Library. Cambridge, MA, 1969.

Wilson, Roger J. A. *Piazza Armerina.* Austin, TX, 1983.

Zohary, Daniel, and Maria Hopf. *Domestication of Plants in the Old World: The Origin and Spread of Cultivated Plants in West Asia, Europe, and the Nile Valley.* Oxford, 1993.

INDEX

ACKNOWLEDGMENTS

I would like to acknowledge Maria Teresa Train and Elizabeth Blair MacDougall for their initial proposal of the book; Mark Greenberg, Editor in Chief, Getty Publications, for agreeing to undertake the project; Benedicte Gilman, Senior Editor, Getty Publications, for guiding the manuscript to publication; Maria Teresa Train for her advice and comprehensive picture research; Abby Sider, for her careful and thorough copy editing of the text; and Kurt Hauser for his accomplished and imaginative design. P. B.

© 2004 J. Paul Getty Trust

Getty Publications
1200 Getty Center Drive, Suite 500
Los Angeles, California 90049-1682
www.getty.edu

Christopher Hudson, Publisher
Mark Greenberg, Editor in Chief

Maria Teresa Train, Photographs Consultant
Abby Sider, Manuscript Editor
Benedicte Gilman, Editorial Coordinator
Kurt Hauser, Designer
Amita Molloy, Production Coordinator
David Fuller, Cartographer
Stephen Harby, Map artist
Diane Franco, Typographer

Printed in Italy by Arti Grafiche Amilcare Pizzi, S.p.A.

Library of Congress Cataloging-in-Publication Data

Bowe, Patrick.
    Gardens of the Roman world / Patrick Bowe.
        p. cm.
Includes bibliographical references (p.   ) and index.
    ISBN 0-89236-740-7 (hardcover)
    1. Gardens, Roman—History. I. Title.
    SB458.55.B68 2004
    712'.0937—dc22

                                2003017143

Half-title page: Discovered in the ancient town of Stabiae near Pompeii and now in the National Archaeological Museum, Naples, this fresco represents the Roman goddess Flora filling her basket with flowers.

Title page: The Roman town of Ephesus in Turkey (see fig. 124).

Page iv: The House of the Vettii, Pompeii (see fig. 90).

Table of Contents (clockwise from top left): Fresco from the House of the Golden Bracelet, Pompeii (see fig. 49); House of the Water Jets, Conimbriga, Portugal (see fig. 156); cloister of the cathedral of Monreale, Sicily (see fig. 164); the Canopus at Hadrian's Villa, Tivoli (see fig. 67).

Page 169: Detail of the herb garden in the Getty Villa, Malibu, California.

This page: Ruins of a Roman villa and its garden in Carthage, Tunisia.